AWAKEN YOUR SOUL

AWAKEN YOUR SOUL

HOW TO FIND YOUR INNER SPIRIT
AND LIFE'S PURPOSE

THEODORE ORENSTEIN

AWAKEN YOUR SOUL
How to Find Your Inner Spirit and Life's Purpose

By Theodore Orenstein

First Edition
Copyright © 2023 by Theodore Orenstein

Life's Purpose Publishing

Paperback ISBN # 978-1-960299-13-0
Hardcover ISBN # 978-1-960299-14-7

Printed in the United States of America

TABLE OF CONTENTS

AUTHOR'S NOTE

I would gratefully like to acknowledge the people who have influenced my life and have greatly contributed to my being able to provide this teaching.

Tyrone Campbell was my first and most profound spiritual teacher. I still live by the principles I learned from him.

Dan Grippo has been by far the best meditation guide I have experienced. His spiritual insight, peaceful nature, and wise teaching overflow to his students, and he remarkably brings very little ego into his teaching. He will recognize many of his teachings in this book, through which I pass them on to others. He can be found at www.as-rayaspirit.com.

Peter Wells, my dear friend, wise companion, and fellow traveler, has given me much valuable inspiration and advice.

Lillian Fruit Orenstein, my mother, will live forever through the love she gave me; which I am passing to my children and to my grand-children, and which I am confident will pass through to future generations.

Louis Orenstein, my father, taught me that one need not be in a religious congregation to connect with God. God is wherever you are.

Beverly Orenstein, my wonderful wife, life companion, and eternal love. It is so easy to feel the Oneness when I am with you.

PREFACE

This book is primarily for those people who have lost or never had, "faith in God," but who are still seeking true meaning and purpose in life; something greater than their daily existence.

I believe I have discovered the ultimate reality which all true religions and spiritual beliefs have at their core. I am writing this book so that I can pass on to you what I have learned and help you attain it yourself. Here I will show you how to receive the revelations I have received.

You may not have previously heard the message I am about to give you, because it is not normally taught by organized religions. However, it is not unique and not novel. I have not invented it. Nothing I am saying here is new. It has been said in various ways throughout history. These ideas have been discovered by countless people since before recorded time. It is your hearing it, really hearing it, that is new. I, myself, believe I have received that revelation that Abraham, Jesus, Buddha, Mohammed, and so many others have received, and it drives me to help others discover it as well.

I am a child of the 20th and 21st centuries. I have found that I do not necessarily connect with books written thousands, or even hundreds of years ago. I also am a rational person who believes in science and history. I cannot accept a belief system that flies in the face of facts that have been discovered by science and history. I cannot believe in miracles which contradict what has been learned about the physical universe.

I have found that the enlightening revelations I have received do not contradict science or my life experience. Through them, I believe

I

I have discovered the spiritual path within me which connects me directly with ultimate reality.

I have learned that all true religious, humanist, and spiritual beliefs at their core contain the same reality. Some may call it higher consciousness, or absolute understanding. Others may call it Nirvana, enlightenment, God, or other names. Once you discover it, names become irrelevant.

It is what it is. It is indescribable, yet more real than anything you have ever experienced.

Hopefully, you are ready to receive the insight I have to share. Everyone is different and is inspired by different messages. I have written this book for those people who have not found higher consciousness through other means, and for those who are aching for greater meaning and purpose in their lives, but are not getting it through the traditional paths that have been offered to them.

I am aware that I am not a recognized religious scholar. For that reason, sometimes in this book when I propose a currently unorthodox concept, I have added quotes from religious and spiritual authorities throughout the ages which support my propositions.

This is not meant to be a scholarly, academic work and I have tried to make this teaching as down-to-earth as possible. It is important to me that this book touches the souls of the widest possible array of people, so I have included wisdom from many diverse viewpoints and cultures. You will see principles and quotes from many different traditions and beliefs, including, among others, those that are Christian, Jewish, Hindu, Taoist, and even those from atheists and humanists.

I am sharing with you what I have learned. I am sharing it heart-to-heart, soul-to-soul. Hopefully, you will find inspiration in my words. I am not spouting some theories I have studied. This teaching comes from my real-life experience.

I refused to use the word God while I was in the midst of enlightenment (when enlightenment was in the midst of me). I felt that in sharing my experience with others, I did not want to trigger their preconceived assumptions and opinions. The word God has separated people from one another for too long. Nonbelievers will close their minds as soon as they hear the word. For some believers, there is only their concept of God and only their way of finding God. Those who don't believe the same way are thought to be heretical, evil, or doomed. Therefore, I was originally not going to use the word God at all in this teaching. I did not want your preconceptions to cloud, or interfere with, your openness to these ideas.

It's funny how words get in the way when people are trying to communicate. People think they disagree with one another merely because they have different definitions of the same word. In this book, I am going to try to show you how to go beyond words and connect directly with your true spirit and that of others.

MY JOURNEY

It was about 3 AM, and I had spent many continuous hours studying for the bar exam in a bare, cold room. It was then that my life changed.

I had an awakening. Through a sudden calm and blissful awareness, I felt a profound and all-encompassing connection to all living things. I suddenly understood completely the spiritual essence of why we should do unto others as we would have them do unto us. Yes, I had heard The Golden Rule repeated all my life, and had always agreed with its premise; but I hadn't previously been awakened to its full depth.

That morning I learned that we do good unto others because we are all fundamentally and totally connected with each other. I am part of you, and you are part of me. At our roots, we are all brothers, sisters, parents, and children of each other. We and all life are one loving family. We are in this together. As we hurt others, we hurt ourselves; and as we help others, we help ourselves. It comes naturally and spontaneously from the love that we all have for one another.

We are connected with each other through a spiritual life force deep within us. It is normally hard to feel because it is subtle and is drowned out by life's daily experiences and necessities. However, if we can ignore life's comings and goings, we can connect with the spirit within us, and its connection with all life.

I understand that these words do not come close to fully describing the realization I had that morning. The reality I discovered cannot be described in words. That is the purpose of this book.

Through this teaching, I use words as a springboard to catapult you to that spiritual existence that is beyond words.

There is a Buddhist saying that when you pick up a hot coal and throw it at another person, you are the one who gets hurt first. Think about it from your own experience. To do a hurtful thing to another, you must already be hurting inside. Don't hate, jealousy, and fear make you seethe within yourself? Don't they make you unhappy?

Harms done to us earlier in life cause us to be driven by anger, jealousy, fear, and other primeval emotions. Those impulses can be so strong that they overpower our true humanity; the fundamental love we have for ourselves and other people. In addition, the deadlines and stresses of life usually prevent us from slowing down and listening to our better selves – our spiritual nature.

You are not your ego. Your ego has been developed over the years through life's painful and happy experiences. Defenses have been built up within you as a result of wrongs that have been done to you. Those defenses are so ingrained within you that you do not see them; you do not even realize they exist. They cause you to react spontaneously and emotionally to people and events. They are primeval survival mechanisms, like fight or flight, which may have been worthwhile in some distant past, but now they usually get in the way. They can be so strong that they overwhelm your true spirit.

Your spirit is the inner essence that connects you with others. If it is allowed to shine, it will show you your life's purpose and will bring you contentment and happiness. You will see beyond your fears, jealousies, and lusts.

How do you find the spirit within you? By looking into your own heart, not outward to the heavens. Within yourself is a deep spiritual commonality with all people, and through that path, you will find spiritual awakening–the ultimate reality. We know it as love.

You get to that spiritual place by feeling, not thinking. Through opening yourself up. When you become open, you make yourself receptive to revelation. That revelation can often come out of despair;

hence the saying, "It is darkest before the dawn." But through the type of prayer called meditation, you can train yourself to open up to your inner spirit and receive revelation without the necessity of deep trauma.

When you escape from day-to-day living and open yourself up, you will receive inspirations, epiphanies, and eventually mind-blowing revelations that will bring you along the road to spiritual awakening. Through that higher consciousness, you will see the true essence of everything and everyone. You will for the first time understand the true meaning of the things which you may have been hearing, or even mouthing to yourself, for years. You will understand the true essence of yourself and of other people.

I have discovered spiritual enlightenment. While the clarity and absoluteness of that understanding may fade from time to time as I traverse day-to-day life, the lessons learned are fundamental and are still within me. That understanding is always in me. It is profound, and having learned it, I cannot forget it. It has changed my life to the core. It has given me a purpose that I did not previously have.

I am an imperfect human being here on Earth; therefore, I am not often in the state of spiritual enlightenment. However, its principles always remain within me. They help me treat people better when I have had a bad day and am stressed. I hope it lessens the occasions when I am sharp or hurtful to others.

As a child, I had a few experiences which might cause one to suspect an aspect of existence beyond that apparent to our six senses. The first time that I remember that overwhelming feeling of oneness with others came when I was about seven or eight years old. I don't exactly remember the events which occasioned it. But I clearly remember that I realized that down deep, I and the other kids were the same, and we wanted the same basic things. It helped me accept my peers, even though I did not always understand their actions.

Again, at about twelve years old, I was deeply troubled that some of the boys had been bullying me. One day, in a flash of understanding, I again came to the same revelation. They were good people within, who had internal problems which caused them to act that way. So, I tried to accept them, and not harbor unnecessary hard feelings within myself.

As a young child, I took seriously what I was taught in religious school. I dutifully listened to the stories and directives. If my Bible fell on the floor, I picked it up and kissed it. I remember doing that. I did it with reverence. But the messages I received as a child, which still stick with me as I traverse life, were the lessons taught to me by my mother when she saw me making unwise decisions: "Two wrongs don't make a right" and "You'll get more with honey than with vinegar."

In junior high school, all of the students had to recite Psalm 23 and The Lord's Prayer at the beginning of every day in homeroom. It is not done anymore because it is thought to impose a certain religious view upon everyone. But as I recited those words every day, I considered them deeply. "Forgive us our trespasses as we forgive those who trespass against us" and "Though I walk through the valley of the shadow of death I will fear no evil." I meditated upon those words and dreamed of what they meant.

Later in my teens, I acquired a cynicism about religion after seeing people going through the motions, reading prayers about a god to which I could not relate, and hearing stories that I could not believe.

In college, I saw myself as an avowed atheist. I loved to debate the issue with believers and discuss it with all others. I coined the phrase, "Man created God in his own image" as a cynical playoff of the Biblical phrase that God created man in his own image. It was my rejection of the humanoid God spoken of in the Bible, described at religious services, and depicted in literature and art. It was my cynical condescension toward the traditional religion I and others around me had been taught.

I did not believe in the god I had heard about all my life. To me, he did not exist. Man had invented it to explain natural phenomena before science could explain them. It seemed logical and obvious to me that man had created God in his own image because of a need to explain natural phenomena. Now that those phenomena had been explained by science, there was no need for God. Even intuitively I could not believe in the god described in the Bible, the humanoid God in the sky who spoke and who became angry, jealous, and forgiving. I did not believe that a super powerful humanoid being had created the world and humankind in six days or had parted the Red Sea.

I believed that a person achieves according to his or her own abilities, wisdom, and luck. There was no God of our prayers helping us. I believed President Kennedy when he said that "Surely God's work on earth must be our own." I rejected the idea of the god that had been taught to me as I grew up. I was, however, still intrigued by the question, and I never tired of discussing it.

In law school, I was the social chairman of my legal fraternity. Father Robert Drinan, a Catholic priest and the Dean of Boston College Law School, was a visiting professor at my school. Still obsessed and still searching for answers (or rather questions), I chose the elective he taught: Law and Religion.

At the time, Madelyn Murray O'Hare, a famous atheist, was living near the law school in Austin, Texas. I tried my best to organize a public debate sponsored by my legal fraternity between Father Drinan and her on the hot subject of abortion. She accepted the invitation, but he declined. I was so looking forward to that debate.

After law school, I was drafted into the U.S. Army. I had much free time in the army and had read many books. One book intrigued me and has stuck in my mind. It was *The Science of Being and Art of Living* by Maharishi Mahesh Yogi. The book tried to describe a transcendent consciousness, but I just didn't get it. He spoke in glowing terms about a state of existence, but I just thought it was vague. I did not understand him. The book was very popular, but I just couldn't make the leap. I apparently was not yet ready to understand his concepts.

In this book I will use concepts that you know and with which you already have a deep connection. I will make it easy for you to join me on this magnificent journey to happiness and profound meaning. To help you along the way, a portion of this book is a practical how-to manual that can be used by logical, rational people to reach transcendent consciousness. It is a consciousness that is not contradicted by logic, yet is not restrained by it.

I spent two years in the Army, and when released on November 6, 1969, I ended up again in Boston where I had grown up. After my discharge from the Army, I began studying for the Massachusetts Bar Examination, which was to take place at the end of December 1969. At the time I was living almost as an ascetic in an insufficiently heated room in a boarding house one very cold winter.

On November 15, 1969, nine days after my Army discharge, I attended the March on Washington against the Vietnam War. At the end of the March, people congregated at the Washington Monument, where there were speeches and singing.

The cast of *Hair*, then on Broadway, sang, "The Dawning of the Age of Aquarius" over and over and over. People were dancing around and holding hands. We thought we were ushering in a new age; an age without war, an age of love.

In the midst of the music, the magical words of that song, the camaraderie of everyone together, our common spirit, and the belief that a new age of love was dawning caused a feeling to creep over me. At the time, I did not identify it as a religious or spiritual experience. All I knew was that it was a wonderful feeling! I was elated. I felt I was part of a larger existence of love. The world was opening and the future was bright.

I went back to Boston after the March and continued studying for the bar exam. On Christmas Eve 1969, I went caroling at Louisburg Square on ancient Beacon Hill in Boston. It is an old Boston tradition. I went to have a cultural, historical, and fun experience.

The quaint Beacon Hill neighborhood dates from the late 1700s. Louisburg Square has always been surrounded by the gracious early Federalist homes of very important and rich people, such as heads of government, business, and society. They have included John

Singleton Copley, Louisa May Alcott, Jack Welch of General Electric, and Senators Edward Kennedy and John Kerry. The ancient tradition calls for the common folk to sing Christmas carols in front of the homes of the aristocracy, and hope for a wave or to be invited in for a drink or a snack.

In the 1950s in our public elementary school, all the kids were taught to memorize and sing Christmas carols irrespective of their religion. I have always loved to sing, and I loved to sing carols. The Christmas season has always made me happy with its spirit of joyous giving. My sister and I looked forward with excitement to every Christmas morning when we would discover and open all of our presents spread on the floor of our living room.

It was in the middle of the night a day or two after I had gone caroling in 1969 when it happened. I was studying for the upcoming bar exam with my soul still buoyed by the spirit of Christmas. It struck me with no warning what Christ meant when he said, "Do unto others as you would have them do unto you." I am within you and you are within me. At our cores, we are one. We are connected through human love. We are one!!! That is why! I am happy when I make others happy, and I am unhappy when I make them unhappy. I know this explanation is not yet enough for you. I will explain it more in length in this book. At that time, it was to me a simple, yet profound, realization. But it would later, through subsequent revelations, become more and more profound.

Prior to that moment, I had been a good, moral person. I had followed the important rules of conduct. I did not lie, cheat, steal, or hurt anyone intentionally. It was at that moment that I first realized the shining spirit behind those rules. It all came together for me. My life was fundamentally changed at that moment. I spread the word to my family and friends. We are one. If I harm you, I harm myself. It struck a chord with a popular phrase at that time, "Don't criticize another man unless you have walked a mile in his moccasins."

I was elated and calm; amazed and filled with quiet contemplation. Everything came together. Everything was understood. I could not fully explain it. It was not explainable in words. It was a revelation! Revelations kept coming to me in the two years following that moment.

I was walking down Beacon Street near Kenmore Square in Boston in the fall of 1970 when I was approached by a person talking about spirituality, and who invited me to a class. Before my revelation of 1969, I would have walked by and ignored that person. I went. I was ready. I was a blossoming flower. I signed up for a "free" session of classes.

Things I would have previously just passed by without notice, I noticed. I craved. I soaked in. They connected with something in me. I was like Moses at the burning bush. If he had not been ready, he would have just passed it by without noticing that the bush was burning and not being consumed. Moses was ready for a revelation, and it came to him.

I learned a major concept in those classes. There was an exercise where we had to sit silently and unmoved while another person taunted us verbally and visually. We had to be calm, silent, and unmoved within. Not even our eyes could move. My body was unmoved in that chair while my mind and spirit were active and filled with awareness. After a while, it felt as if I were somehow separate from my body, and I was witnessing it sitting in that chair.

I learned from that exercise that I am not my body. I am a spirit that resides within this body in order to exist in, and therefore interact with, this physical world. That is an important lesson to learn. The grandeur, and seemingly endless reaches of the Gothic cathedrals of Catholicism, are made to encourage your spirit to soar upward and outward beyond your body.

At about the same time I had that experience, without warning or preparation, I had a direct connection with the spark of life within me. During this moment in my life, I was living in a one-bedroom apartment with four other people. I had very little money. I ate old cheap cold cuts for a time and was a vegetarian for a while. I was learning and experimenting with life. It was during that period that without warning or feeling, a spiritual awakening came over me. I recognized it at the time as what some call Nirvana, enlightenment, or a direct connection to God. It lasted about thirty-six hours.

During that period, I understood everything. All was crystal clear to me. I recognized it as being connected to the feeling I had at the 1969 March on Washington, and the revelation I had after Christmas caroling soon thereafter. The wondrous feeling left as quickly as it had appeared, but the lessons learned stayed with me. We are one!

Soon after that, my friend Paul and I were walking down Cambridge Street next to Beacon Hill toward the Charles River Esplanade on the way to an outdoor music concert. We passed a group of people on the sidewalk and started talking with them. In that group was the man who would become my first spiritual teacher, Tyrone Campbell.

Somehow, we began talking about spirituality. He seemed wise to me. I remember he called me an old soul. He invited us to visit him and his family at his apartment. We took him up on it a few days later. He was a Buddhist and had studied with a learned teacher. A group of people had gathered around him, and informal sessions were held in his living room pretty much every night. The discussions were very deep. I had never before been in such an environment. I had many questions. I learned so much.

I moved out of the apartment in Harvard Square where I had been living, and I moved into Tyrone's apartment where he lived with his wife and two-year-old daughter. My bed was a mattress in a corner of his living room.

Every night people gathered around and had discussions about spirituality, life, meaning, and the very nature of understanding. That revelatory feeling came back to me. The feeling of being at one with all living things, with the entire universe. Pure infinite awareness. With it came an innate understanding of why people are what they are. It was not an understanding in the nature of an intellectual understanding, but more of a transcendental spiritual awareness.

I was entirely in that Nirvana experience for about three weeks. I developed a philosophy of life during that time, which has kept evolving over the years. It is the philosophy contained in this book. But it is probably wrong to call it a philosophy. A philosophy tends to be intellectual and is described with words. Although those discussions in Tyrone's home were discussions using words, those words were an attempt to describe a feeling, an existence, an essence that went far beyond the power of words to describe. So, although I use words in this book, I intend these words to catapult you to a level of understanding beyond words.

During that wondrous time, I called my experience, "Absolute Understanding." Others call it Universal Consciousness, which I think is a better definition. It is also called, among other things, Nirvana, enlightenment, Complete Submission, and God.

Through Universal Consciousness, I understood others so completely that it was as if I were understanding myself completely. Through that understanding of others, I gained a greater understanding of myself. It goes hand in hand. For example, I realized that the human spirit is eternal, that there is a purpose and direction to the universe, and that it is good. I also realized that there is a purpose to life. That in fact, life is just too profound to be meaningless.

I learned that life's substance is love, that love is the answer to all, and that Absolute Love is the true reality. I learned that when within Absolute Love, all is automatically known and there is no doubt. With it came the realization that such an awareness has always been within me, within all people, and that all one has to do is open to one's spirituality within one's self. Even though such a revelation cannot last indefinitely in this imperfect lifetime on earth, it cannot be forgotten or doubted. It changes one's life.

I eventually came to understand that Absolute Understanding, universal consciousness, Absolute Love, and universal love are all descriptions of the same thing. This will be more completely explained in this book.

After I had obtained spiritual enlightenment, I remember thinking to myself that I had finally, after all these years, discovered my eternal spirit, and therefore it would be alright if my body died. I also decided that since I had learned to know myself, I was ready to have children.

I have recently read *Cosmic Consciousness* [1] by Richard Maurice Bucke. Mr. Bucke studied the writings and sayings of many famous people throughout history and gives examples through quotations showing that they achieved the same kind of higher consciousness I am describing here. He describes those people as receiving "sudden illumination, joy, and all-knowingness." Among the people he gives as examples, and from whom he submits quotations, are Jesus, Buddha, Mohammed, Paul the Apostle, Walt Whitman, Roger Bacon, Moses, Gideon, Isaiah, Socrates, Benedict Spinoza, William Wordsworth, and Ralph Waldo Emerson. But Universal Consciousness is not just for the famous. It has come to me, and it can come to you.

Mr. Bucke also reports from his studies that each of those people throughout history who achieved spiritual enlightenment had experienced it one to three times during their lifetime. As with my experiences, it was not permanent, but it did change their lives. In hindsight, I can now see that my epiphanies have been necessary steps along the path to spiritual awakening: my realization in the early morning of December 1969 that love is the answer to all; my realization at the sessions I attended in Cambridge that I am not my body, but am a spirit inhabiting my body in order to operate within this physical world; my entrance into a world of wonder while living with Tyrone; and the recognition at a later moment when sitting in my car that I must bring my realizations to the world, and not become an isolated monk.

I can now also see that each successive revelation brought me one more dimensional step closer to spiritual enlightenment. In December 1969, it was revealed to me that I am not separate from my fellow human beings. That at our cores, they and I are the same, and that love is the connection between us. In 1970, I realized that I am not my body; it is merely my vehicle, and that my existence is universal, not limited by the edges of my physical body or by its lifespan. In 1971, while living with Tyrone, I entered that Universal Consciousness known by many as God, Nirvana, or spiritual enlightenment. In that state, I realized that Absolute Love is the essence of existence and is the only true reality. That when experiencing Absolute Love all is known, there is no desire and no need, that it has always been within us, and that it can be found by anyone opening one's self up to it. It is so absolutely profound that it is greater than our physical lives.

Finally, while sitting in my car in March of 1971, during that period when I was living with Tyrone, I saw that my purpose was to stay within the world and practice what I had learned. It was even later, probably in the later 1970s, that I found that I have a mission: to teach others what I have learned. That was when I began recording what I had learned. Now, forty-plus years later, I am ready to bring it out into the world.

I have now read many books about religion and spirituality, but I have not been able to connect with some of them. Those written by academics can be dry and technical, so they are difficult with which to relate. Those by religious or spiritual leaders are often written from the narrow standpoint of their beliefs and may even use their internal lingo. It has been hard for me, an outsider, to relate to the message they are trying to communicate. That is why I have tried to make this book, not only inspiring but as down to earth and as broadly focused as possible. I want people of all backgrounds, experiences, and levels of understanding to be able to easily relate to what I am trying to say.

This teaching will not only be helpful to disillusioned nonbelievers. It will also be helpful to those who have followed the rules and traditions of their inherited religion but still have not found happiness and life's true meaning. This book can also be helpful to those people who feel satisfied that they already have a direct connection to God. Through the ideas and techniques presented here, you may find an even deeper, more profound understanding of God, and how to better stay connected with your true spirit. My way may not be yours. Take what is helpful from this teaching and travel your own way. If you truly do connect with God, your higher consciousness, pursue it and perfect it. We will eventually meet in the same place.

I do not want you to take my teaching only upon faith. That is why I have included techniques through which you, through regular practice, can yourself connect with your inner spiritual light. The words in this book are here in an attempt to catapult you to a dimension that words cannot describe. To an existence beyond your day-to-day earthly world. To an existence, which is within you, but which cannot be fully conceptualized by your thinking brain. I have tried to translate eternal concepts into the language of the present so that you can personally identify with those concepts. Hopefully, through that identification, you will open your heart to the eternal ideal.

But I try to do more. I discovered in my previous professional life that I have the ability to take esoteric concepts and present them in a way with which people can directly identify. I can take what seems like formidably difficult tasks and break them down into simple steps that make them easy to follow and apply. Through the time-proven contemplative practices described here, you, through dedication and patience, will be able to gradually open yourself up to your core of inner peace and inspiration where you can find your spiritual light. I have not intended to write a work of literature. I have tried to write a book of inspiration and instruction that is easy to approach and can be applied by anyone. Let's do it.

FINDING SPIRITUAL ENLIGHTENMENT

You probably think you know what God is, and based on that definition of God, you either believe in God or not. Let me guess. That definition of God was devised by someone else, not you.

Who says you have to accept someone else's idea of God? Who says that God is in the sky and speaks with a thunderous voice with lightning and thunder? Who decided that you can ask an outside entity for miracles, and that "He" can grant them if you follow his dictates?

Have you said to yourself that you cannot really believe that a god parted the Red Sea, created the universe in six days, cured blindness with a touch, or brought people back to life? Wouldn't it be nice to believe in a god that is believable?

You do not have to accept any of those concepts of God. You do not have to accept anyone else's idea of God. Any God which does not touch you personally and directly, and does not affect you deeply, is not your God! You are correct to not believe in such a god.

We each have our own path to walk and no one can do it for us. The nature of spiritual enlightenment, or God, is that you must find it yourself. If you do not find God yourself, you have not found it. A teacher or guide can help you along the way, but it is you who must ultimately connect directly with your pure inner spirit.

Who am I to tell you this? Why should you listen to me?

I am a creature of logic as well as of spirit. If I am to believe something, it must not be contrary to my life experience. In my college days and beyond, until my own spiritual awakening, I considered myself an atheist. I now believe in God but have not changed my requirement that God does not contradict science, history, and life's experience. The difference, I have learned through hindsight, is that my problem was that I had accepted the definition of God taught to me by others, and therefore was forced to either reject such a god or suspend experience.

I have now discovered God and I have been surprised to learn that the god I have discovered is the same transcendental Universal Love that is at the heart of the beliefs of enlightened Jews, Christians, Islamists, Hindus, Buddhists, humanists, atheists, and enlightened people of every age and place. Some call it God, and some do not, but it is the same.

The operative word is love. At the heart of the beliefs of the enlightened of all of the Earth's great religions and non-religious spiritual and philosophical beliefs is the same thing. It is just expressed in different words and seen through the prism of different cultures and times.

I have discovered that God is a dimension within me.

In order to believe in God, which can also be called oneness or spiritual enlightenment, there is no need to suspend reason and experience. However, that does not mean that God must be fully explained by reason and experience. Just because you have not yet experienced something, does not mean it does not exist.

Imagine that you are an aboriginal person living in a tribe deep in the Amazon. You have not yet had contact with the outside world. If an explorer were to come upon you and tell you that there are invisible words and images flying through the air all around you, would you believe him? You have never experienced such a thing in your life but perhaps there have been occasions when you have not realized that something existed before having encountered it yourself. Could it be that you have just not yet become sensitized to experiencing those invisible sounds and images? By obtaining a television with an antenna, you are then able to see and hear what had been there all along.

Could it be that there is a part of you which, if trained, could sense or "see" a power, or existence, which you have not yet been able to sense? After all, we have barely scratched the surface of our understanding of the brain.

So, how do you as a rational person see, and perhaps even enter, a spiritual world not restrained by logic, yet not contradicted by it? An inspired Jewish prayer on Yom Kippur, the holiest day of the Jewish year, says: "O God, how can we know You? Where can we find You? You are as close to us as breathing, yet You are farther than the farthermost star. You are as mysterious as the vast solitudes of night, yet as familiar to us as the light of the sun." [1] How can we begin to sense a yet undiscovered something that is as close to us as breathing, and as familiar to us as the light of the sun?

WHAT IS GOD?

God Is Love

What does God feel like? God can be felt in many ways and at many levels, depending on who you are and where you are in life. Almost all of us have felt God at one time or another without realizing it.

Have you heard that God is love? Through parental or romantic love have you ever loved a person with such purity and unconditional completeness that you totally accepted them without reservation, received your happiness through their happiness, and would have gladly sacrificed yourself for them? When in the midst of that love, did you feel that it transcended physical life itself? Have you ever been happier than in the midst of that love? Then you have experienced God.

Although you cannot fully explain true love through intellectual reasoning, you don't let reasoning deny it for you, do you? And so it is with God!

That experience of God through romantic or parental love is a mere glimpse of what God, or spiritual enlightenment, is, and can be for you. When you feel a love of that purity and totality <u>for all beings</u>, you will be within spiritual enlightenment, God, your true spirit. Love is natural within you. It sits at the center of your being. True absolute love needs nothing. It is complete all by itself.

You can experience spiritual enlightenment with total understanding and total clarity. When you have such a profound innate love and understanding of the universe and its beings, you literally, naturally, automatically, understand others to the core, and see the often-hidden goodness within them. Love allows you to connect with others in spite of differences you may have with them. You recognize yourself in them. You, yourself, are not always the best person you can be, but hopefully, others will still accept you and like you.

Isn't it interesting how we accept character defects in our family, friends, and loved ones, which we would not accept in strangers? What if we loved all humankind the way we love those close to us? If you assume the best in people, you may find it. If you assume the worst, you will likely find <u>that</u>. You may have a close friend or relative who does not have a very good personality. Even though people who do not know him or her, may not like that person, and may feel that he or she is brash, loud, arrogant, or selfish, you see through that to the truly good person within, don't you?

Now imagine if you spontaneously felt that toward strangers and people who have harmed you. That comes from the inspiration of spiritual enlightenment, or God. It is the universal love, the unconditional love, that allows you to see the core goodness of all and love them as brothers and sisters.

What a way to walk through this world! You would be "in the spirit of God."

You would understand others so completely that you would see yourself in them, weaknesses and all. You would be "at One" with them. Feelings of selfishness, jealousy, retribution, anger, and other "sins" stem from the feeling that you are separate from other people. You will become enlightened when you see that fundamentally they are you and you are them.

You will see that others are imperfectly trying to make their way in this world, just as you are. That will cause you to empathize with them and be naturally drawn to feel goodness toward them. Sure, they have come from, and see the world through different cultures and different life experiences. But you can think of them as you think of yourself: trying to do the best you can in spite of your limitations.

Feeling love for them will make you feel good, just as feeling self-ishness, hate, or retribution toward them will make you feel unhappy within yourself. Remember the Buddhist saying that feeling anger toward another person is like picking up a hot coal and throwing it at them? You are the one who is hurt first.

So, the Word of God is not a booming voice dictating from on high, but really is a profound feeling you experience while you are within the Oneness which connects you with all. Perhaps this concept of God will let you see those old religious teachings with new eyes.

This is not a new concept. I have not created it. This concept has been known since before recorded time and has been proposed by enlightened people of every culture and age.

Here are some familiar examples of the Word of God. You can see how they are inspired by the feeling of love for all people.

"And a stranger shalt thou not oppress; for ye know the heart of a stranger seeing ye were strangers in the land of Egypt." —Exodus 23:9

"'Love your neighbor as yourself. I am the LORD.'" —Leviticus 19:18

About 100 years before Jesus, there lived a famous rabbi named Hillel the Elder. Rabbi Hillel was the most respected rabbi of his time and is one of the most respected rabbis in the history of Judaism.

Rabbi Hillel, voicing the inspiration received from the Holy Spirit within him, summarized the Jewish faith by saying, "What is hateful to thee, do not unto thy fellow man: this is the whole Law; the rest is mere commentary" (Shab. 31a). Love is the source of Judaism.

Jesus was apparently a follower of Hillel's teachings because he connected with and repeated Hillel's summation, but he did improve upon it by putting it in the positive. He created a mandate to do good rather than to just avoid doing bad. A sending of humanity out to improve the world: "Do to others what you want them to do to you. This is the meaning of the law of Moses and the teaching of the prophets" (Matthew 7:12).

John said: "Anyone who claims to be in the light but hates a brother or sister is still in the darkness. Anyone who loves their brother and sister lives in the light, and there is nothing in them to make them stumble."

Confucius in 500 B.C. said: "Never do to others what you would not like them to do to you." [1]

The famous Native American proverb says the same thing in another way: "Do not criticize a man until you've walked a mile in his moccasins."

The Golden Rule is golden because it is really all that has to be understood. As Hillel would say, all else is commentary.

You can easily, naturally, and automatically follow The Golden Rule and love your neighbor as yourself. You do it by feeling Universal Love, feeling at One with all people. If you are experiencing Universal Love, it just comes naturally.

"If you think you understand the scriptures, but it does not build love of God and neighbor, then you don't understand." —Origen of Alexandria

Islam tells you not to follow your petty urges, or the emotions drawing you to hatred, jealousy, retaliation, or greed. It teaches that following the Godly path is identifying with another person. "That which joins us all, that is the connection of us all," —from the mouth of the Imam of Al Aqsa Mosque. [2]

"... Love is the only force capable of transforming an enemy into a friend. We never get rid of an enemy by meeting hate with hate; we get rid of an enemy by getting rid of enmity. By its very nature, love creates and builds up. Love transforms with redemptive power." — Martin Luther King.

The Devi Bhagavatam, one of the holy books of India, says, "Love is the manifestation of it. For when truly loving a person, a thing, a concept, we become a part of it, and it is a part of us." [3] So, the answer is to become One with others.

As you expand your world of love so that you love increasingly greater spheres of humanity, and then love all spheres of life, you become closer and closer to the universal oneness. Then, when you are all and all is you, you will be awakened. Your consciousness will be limitless and you will become aware that everything in the universe is encompassed within this moment in which you exist. Every moment in which you exist. As illustrated previously, you already know love. God is love, so love can be your doorway to God.

God Is One

In Hinduism there is a Vedic saying: Truth is one, but scholars speak of it in many ways." [4]

Confucius said "... In the world there are many different roads, but the destination is the same."[5]

In Taoism: "There are a hundred deliberations, but the result is one." [6]

"One love, One heart. Let's get together and feel alright." From "One Love" by Bob Marley and Curtis Mayfield.[7]

The One Being, of him who his sages call by many names. [8]

One of the most important Jewish prayers speaks directly about how becoming one with others is the way of God, and provides the method for achieving it: "O may all, created in Your image, become One in spirit and One in friendship, forever united in Your service. Then shall Your kingdom be established on earth." (emphasis supplied) [9]

So, now we may begin to understand why the Bible says that man is created in God's image. Not visually and physically, but spiritually. It teaches us that we as humans are a part of the Oneness, the Holy Spirit – "God.".

The "Shema," the fundamental watchword of the Jewish faith, declares: "Hear O Israel. The Lord thy God, the Lord is One."[10] Loosely translated it means: Hey, people of Israel, listen to me! God is One! ("You are wondering what God is? God is the Oneness of all.")

Some translations of the Bible recite the second sentence of the Shema as "The LORD our God is one LORD." That translation, though true, misses the greater point. The lesser point is that there is only one God. The greater point is that God is All and that All is One.

Consider when it was written, and what Jews believed at that time. At that time, Jews did not believe that there was only one god. They believed that their god, the god called Yahweh, was more powerful than the gods of the Canaanites, Mesopotamians, Egyptians, and other peoples. Contemporary biblical passages accept the existence of those other gods. Exodus 20:3, 34:15, and 34:16; Deuteronomy 6:14, 12:30, 12:31, 29:26, and 32:17; Numbers 25:2; Judges 2:12 and 10:16; Joshua 24:15; and Chronicles 25:14 and 28:23; among others. Just consider the second commandment: "Thou shalt have no other gods before me." Genesis 20:1-3. In other words, there <u>are</u> other gods, but you shall not put them before me.

Abraham did originate the concept of one god for his followers. But at the time of the Old Testament, the Jews lived in Mesopotamia, Canaan, and in Egypt. It was a world where it was assumed that there were many gods. The belief in multiple gods was so ingrained in society as a whole, that the Jews agreed to disagree. The others could have the gods they wanted, but the Jews had one god, and he was more powerful than the rest.

Since contemporary biblical passages accepted the existence of other gods in other religions, how can we interpret the meaning of the Shema to mean that at that time they believed that there was only one god in all of existence? That would contradict their own biblical passages.

If the people who wrote "God is One," also believed that there were other gods, then how could they have meant that there was only one god? They did not yet believe it themselves. They had one god, but they also acknowledged that gods existed in other religions.

Some religious scholars may disagree, however, their interpretation misses the point that the spiritually inspired writers of the Shema are trying to tell us. It is the same truth that wise, inspired people of all religions and spiritual people of no religion have been trying to teach us for millennia. The Shema does not merely mean that there is only one god, it means what it says: God is One. Why can't we take them simply for their word? That truth may have been lost in time by people who had not yet connected with their own spirituality, but YOU can discover it for yourself, just as the inspired writers of the Shema did.

In further support of this interpretation of the biblical passage, I submit two other proclamations:

1. "Unto thee it was shewed, that thou mightest know that the LORD he is God; there is none else beside him."—Deuteronomy IV:35.

"None else." Not: "there is no other God beside him." There is nothing, NOTHING, beside him.

2. "Know therefore this day, and consider it in thine heart, that the LORD he is God in heaven above, and upon the earth beneath: there is none else."—Deuteronomy IV:39.

They say "there is none else" and "there is none else beside him." Not "there are no other gods beside him." There is nothing besides him. Nothing. Not in heaven and not upon the earth. Nothing. How clearer could it be?

Maimonides, perhaps the greatest Jewish philosopher of all time, said in the 12th century: "God is one ... in a manner that surpasses any unity that is found in the world. i.e. He is not one in the manner of a general category which includes many individual entities, nor one in the way that a body is divided into different portions and dimensions. Rather, he is unified, and there exists no unity similar to his in this world..." [11]

Here is the best analogy I have ever encountered comparing the Oneness within us to our self-concept as an individual: "The wave awakens to the awareness that it is water; its true origin. Water raises the waves and goes over them at the same time. There are many different kinds of waves, different forms, but water has neither form nor difference; water is homogeneous and formless and yet the origin of waves of all forms. Waves form and vanish, but water is eternal and indestructible, and it remains so even when it appears and disappears." [12] At the heart of all waves is water. Water is the oneness that is common to and connects all waves.

"Looking deeply means observing something or someone with so much concentration that the distinction between the observer and the observed disappears. The result is insight into the true nature of the object." [13]

Becoming one with others in this earthly world of individual personalities does not mean that you merge your identity with another and lose your own personality. It means you learn to see beyond both your personalities, learn to fully accept one another and not judge the other. It means you develop the ability to feel each other's misery and happiness, and that you completely accept and confirm the humanity of each other.

The Roman Cicero said: "When each person loves the other as much as himself, it makes one out of many." [14]

Even Karl Marx, a famous atheist, said he believed that the mission of communism was "the advent of the Brotherhood of Man" where all people should come together as one in mutual assistance.

When you can have such a relationship, you are on the path to Oneness. The more that you can have such a relationship with greater and greater circles of beings, the closer you come to the essence of The One–spiritual enlightenment, Nirvana–God.

Your spirit can channel an existence that is greater than you. It is unformed pure awareness. Your spirit was here before you arrived as an individual, and will exist after your individual life ceases to exist.

What is within The One? The purity of pure being, luminous clarity, and compassion.

Everything is an inseparable part of The One. When you realize that truthfully, you will be fully enlightened. Consider a chair. When enlightened, you can look at a chair and see the entire universe. There was the seed of the oak which fell upon the soil, the rain and the sun which caused it to grow to the oak from which came the wood. There were the volcanoes that created the vein of iron ore from which the miner extracted the iron for the screws, the people working at the smelter, the carpenters, those truckers, and all of their ancestors whose lines culminated in them. If you can look at that chair and truly see the entire universe, then you can attain spiritual enlightenment, the awareness of the Oneness of all. To see One in all and all in One means you have broken through the great barrier of the perception of reality, of life.

If you can see The One within everything and everybody, how can you feel lonely, jealous, or selfish? Jealous of what? Yourself? For you will know that you are inseparable from all. How can you be selfish once you know that to deprive someone else is to deprive yourself? For to lessen a part of the inseparable universe is to lessen yourself.

We are all in this together. Your life has no limits and no boundaries. You are a part of everyone else. The idea that you are separate and that you gain at someone else's loss is merely an illusion. It is the illusion born of matter, but as the matter has evolved into a human being with the capability to conceptualize of a life beyond its mere physical vehicle, its body, you can break through the barrier encompassing that illusion of separateness. As human beings, we have grown in wisdom to the point where we can make that leap of perception to the universality of life. It has taken us millions of years and we are now on the threshold of the universal reality of pristine awareness.

It has been within us all along. It is within the mother bird which protects its newborn babies. It is that inborn instinctual love that exists in even lower forms of animal life and, who knows, perhaps even within plant life.

Here we are. We have lived on this physical plane for eons, taking the good and the bad, and undergoing natural selection until we have developed into beings able to transcend that next step of evolution. That step which takes us beyond the reality of the physical to the reality of the spiritual, the dimension where there are no boundaries, where there are no relativities. The universal.

It has been within you since your ancestor was a basic form of life. At first imperceivable, and then gradually becoming more and more perceptible over the eons. It is that inborn instinct that is love. Let it develop within you into Universal Love, the Love of all. Connecting to all with all your being; the full realization of life.

Gravity draws things toward one another. Even very solid objects are made up of mostly empty space. Their atoms have vast spaces between neutrons, protons, and electrons, but there is a powerful force holding them all together. Molecules are also bound together by a force. The all-encompassing force that permeates the physical universe is the force of unity. Everything is drawn or bound together by a fundamental force. At the animal level, and especially at the human level, that force could be described as a form of love. Do you disagree that the force that binds humans together is a form of love in love's broadest, and perhaps greatest sense?

I recently watched a program on public television about the beginnings of the universe. It was narrated by a physics professor. I have since read a transcript of classes taught by another physics professor on the same subject. They were fascinating and connected with the theme of this book. They said that the universe just after the Big Bang was an intensely hot soup of swirling individual protons, electrons, and neutrons rushing about in all directions and bouncing off of one another. It only lasted a few seconds.

The universe almost immediately started cooling off and the protons and neutrons slowed down enough so that their gravitational pulls became stronger than the energy of the Big Bang. When they then came close to one another, they drew one another in through the force of gravity. By doing so they formed hydrogen atoms, helium atoms, and other light elements. Eventually, the hydrogen and helium atoms themselves were drawn together through gravity, and as more and more of them drew together they formed stars.

A few of those stars became gigantic and had such a great density that their great gravitational field pulled more and more atoms into them causing them to become denser and denser, which increased their temperature. The fierce closeness of the atoms and the higher temperature caused them to fuse into more complex atoms such as carbon and water. Eventually, those gigantic stars became so dense that they exploded, becoming supernovas and throwing all of those smaller and more complex atoms into the universe.

Ultimately through gravitational pull, groups of stars gathered together into galaxies. Those galaxies were comprised of suns and clouds of gas. The clouds of gas included the more complex atoms which were eventually drawn together by each of their own gravitational pulls to form planets. Some of the planets were close to the suns and were very hot, others were much further away from their suns and were very cold. Our planet Earth is just the right distance, so the complex atoms were then drawn together through gravity and sunlight to form primitive cells which lived in the great sea. The sun reacts with water and carbon atoms through photosynthesis to form life. Those cells eventually grew to use the sun's light to recreate themselves through that process of photosynthesis. Photosynthesis also creates oxygen which nurtures other forms of life.

The point I am trying to make here is that gravity is the force common to everything in our universe. It permeates the entire universe. Gravity draws everything together. Each neutron and electron has a gravitational force, as does every complex form of life. Gravity is causing everything in the universe to eventually unite. Could it be that gravity is the most basic form of love that is moving us all toward The One? Toward unity?

WHERE DO WE LOOK TO FIND THAT ONENESS?

"Oh God, how do we know you? Where can we find you? You are as close to us as breathing, yet you are farther than the farthest star. You are as mysterious as the vast solitudes of night, yet as familiar to us as the light of the sun." [1]

Where could the thing be that is as close to us as breathing and as familiar to us as the light of the sun? It is within us.

If you want to search for the meaning of life, for the ultimate reality, be prepared for a journey into yourself. Into the deepest part of you, where your ego disappears and you can see yourself in all other living things. You will find the source of life. You will become spiritually enlightened. That is where God–your pure spirit, Nirvana–your Absolute Understanding is. That is your "Oneness." If you go far enough within yourself, you will connect with all creation.

The depth within yourself where you find your connection to The One is not depth in the sense of depth below. It is deep in the sense of depth within, but not physically within. It is in the depth of your being, your soul. Like the expression "deep within your heart." That expression obviously does not mean that it is physically within your heart. It is deeper than any physical aspect of yourself. It is spiritual. It is a wiping away of your shell of self-concept, your ego, to unveil your illuminated spiritual inner nature.

Once you have found the Oneness within you, you will know that it permeates all depths. It permeates all. It is the essence of all, from the highest to the lowest. It will become the essence of all you think, and all you do.

Is there an innate drive to unite? Atoms unite into molecules,

molecules into organisms, and organisms into families. Humans love and protect their children forming nuclear families, then they expand the circle of unity to include cousins, then villages, city-states, nations, and then to our present state of globalism. The ever-proceeding unification of life.

As human beings, the highest form of physical life, we are even drawn to something higher. We have the ability to conceive of an existence beyond the physical level of our existence, further toward our unification with our life source. Toward that existence which has an absolute understanding of all forms of existence, and knows that it encompasses all forms of existence. Where within that pure being-ness we automatically love all and know the basis of all. Spiritual awakening leads us to that final evolutionary leap.

Since it is absolute love, love will be at the essence of all you say, and all you do. And, as it is said in the holy books of all paths, you will be a blessing unto the world. Buddha and Jesus knew that the great eternal is within you, and not in some heaven above and outside of you. The Buddha taught, "Look within, thou art the Buddha." While Jesus taught, "The Kingdom of Heaven is within you."

Jesus himself shows us that even a common person such as a carpenter can find God within him or herself. The spirit of God, also known as spiritual enlightenment, is within every one of us and we all can find it.

Buddha was born a prince, son of a king. When his first-born child was an infant, he left his arranged marriage and became an ascetic to seek the meaning of life. He gave up earthly pleasures, food, and good clothes. He underwent pain. He wandered the woods and villages, but could not find the answer. He asked monks for the meaning of life but did not receive satisfactory answers. He eventually learned that such knowledge could not be learned by seeking something outside of himself. It is not some great mystery. He learned that the truth and wisdom a man seeks, he can find within himself, within his own soul. [2]

"All know the Way, but few actually walk it."–Buddha

You can try to get away from it all – to find peace and happiness in the country, or at the beach. What you will come to realize is that you can have it any time you like by going within. Heaven can be found in the quiet of your own awareness.

Karen Armstrong is one of the foremost religious historians of our time. Through her in-depth studies of all religions and their histories, she has come to certain conclusions. She says: "Men and women have a potential for the divine, and are not complete unless they realize it in themselves." [3]

"The traveler has to knock at every alien door to come to his own, and one has to wander through all the outer worlds to reach the innermost shrine at the end. My eyes strayed far and wide before I shut them and said 'Here art thou!' The question and the cry 'Oh, where?' melt into tears of a thousand dreams and change the world with the flood of the assurance – 'I am!'" [4]

St. Augustine's description of God from *Confessions*, VII, io, is: "I entered into my inward self, thou being my guide ... And I beheld with the eye of my soul, above my mind, the Light unchangeable! It was not the ordinary light which all flesh may look upon, nor is it a greater of the same kind ... He who knows the truth knows that Light, and he who knows it knows Eternity." Notice that he says he sensed the eye of his soul which was "above" his mind, beyond his mind. There he "saw" a brilliance and clarity which he says was like a light, but not like any light "which all flesh may look upon." He was referring to a clarity beyond any physical sense.

Plotinus, the Hellenistic philosopher, said in his writings to Flaccus: "You can only comprehend the infinite by a faculty superior to reason, by entering into a state in which you are your finite self no longer—in which the divine essence is communicated to you. This is ecstasy. It is in the liberation of the mind from finite consciousness." [5]

Martin Luther, one of the founders of Christian Protestantism, was reading a psalm that was very familiar to him when those words cut into him like a knife. He then received a revelation that changed him: "Suddenly I saw a new meaning in those words. It was like a light bulb turning on. Suddenly I saw the full meaning of those words." [6]

Martin Luther through that revelation realized that righteousness is achieved, not through doing good deeds, but is found through love. Through love, you are naturally, automatically drawn to good toward others.

John Calvin, another founder of Protestantism, said that it is not through human reasoning that one gains truth about God, but through a direct experience of God. He believed, as did many in Christianity, that man is by nature corrupt and evil, and only through the grace of God or Christ can man find salvation and goodness. [7]

You will discover that the "grace of God" can be found within yourself; within all people. That the corruption and wrong deeds of people come from their ego, and that the control that it has over one's soul can be neutralized through your discovery of your Oneness with all people which has always been within you.

So, it is your surface ego which the Christians say is evil, and it is your inner oneness that they call the grace of God. The "grace of God" is also called Nirvana, The One, cosmic consciousness, and by other names by different people with different beliefs at different times. But it is the same thing. There is only one Oneness, and it is within all of us. We just have to allow ourselves to feel it, to "see" it as the Bible says.

Even humanism and communism can be paths to that same mountaintop. The greatest proponents of humanism accepted this concept of One. Hegel proposed that the world is the product of an "Absolute Mind, distinct from individual minds, but containing them within itself. The stuff of reality, then, is spiritual rather than material." [8] Even Feuerbach, who thought that Hegel was making humanism too religious, said, "Man first sees his nature as if <u>outside</u> of himself before he finds it in himself." He considered the ultimate human experience to be the full awareness of one's self. [9] Does that sound familiar? Man's "nature" is the spiritual essence within himself.

Even the supposedly atheistic communists agreed that the utopian ideal would come from the love within us. Karl Marx charged that religion was "the opiate of the people," but he himself envisioned a utopian communist society where people could exercise and develop their talents to the fullest and people would come together in brotherhood, and out of such pure love would come his utopian vision.[10] It seems that the humanists and atheists are rejecting religion, but not God as set forth in this teaching.

The further you go into the essence at the depths of yourself, the more you expand to others. That is because the unity with all things is so far within you that it is at your common denominator with all beings. It is not a physical common denominator like atoms, it is a spiritual connection which is part of a greater universal spirit. The One is a part of time and space, but it is far greater. It is beyond time and space yet is at the very essence of all times and all spaces.

Maharishi Mahesh Yogi teaches that The One is pure being; the state of pure existence; life itself. He says that "everything is the expression of pure existence or absolute being; which is the essential constituent of all relative life." "Relative life" is life in the physical universe. He says that God has two forms: one is absolute and eternal and the other "takes on the phenomenal existence of various things." At its source, God or Pure Being is absolute and pure, and it radiates into the relative universe. The farther it radiates from pure being, the further it transforms into relative life, the bright light getting dimmer and dimmer.

The point where you begin to see beyond relativity is the open window through which your spirit can experience the wonder of Pure Being, a state unlike anything we have ever before known. It is unlike anything in our known relativistic dualistic world.

How and why spirit began transforming into our relativistic physical universe I certainly do not know. What I do know is that the closer you get to experiencing The One, the more your worldly barriers to pure wisdom are shed until the point where you can see through that window. At that point, your life instantly becomes released from its egoistic existence and you experience enlightenment. When you get to that place within you, you identify with all beings, because all beings are essentially one spirit at their substance.

Your unity with all life is your true natural state. The One, the unity of all life, is found at your spiritual core. The One within you is a part of the universal One, which is All. The One within you is your connection with the unity between you and all other life. It is that which connects all life, that which is common among all life, and that which makes all of life one big loving family. Know that your heart is an inseparable part of the great heart of life. Think of God as an ocean and you as a drop of water within it. You are tiny by yourself, yet mighty when joined with all the other drops that make up the ocean. Do not continue to conceive of yourself as only a single drop. Open your eyes.

That connection is where you will find spiritual enlightenment—God, Allah, The Light, Oneness, The Word, Ultimate Reality, Cosmic Consciousness, Nirvana, The Force, or whatever you want to call it. In that place, words and names mean nothing. It is without belief or creed. It is where all life is unified; it is the Oneness of all.

That place is a pure unadulterated part of you which has a direct understanding of your true nature and of the nature of life. A complete sense of your being arises from that understanding. Once you find your inner spirit, The One, you will see the inner nature of all things. It is an experience which brings amazement, calmness, clarity, and a natural absolute knowingness.

When you absolutely understand everything, you love everything. How can you not? You see that you and everything are One at the most profound level. You, therefore, love all as you love yourself, and through loving all absolutely you love yourself absolutely. Love is the profound lifeforce or level of existence which connects all things. It is at the root of all. It is Oneness of all.

That connection exists within and without the physical universe. It permeates the physical universe and is the way to transcend the physical universe. When you feel Absolute Love, you are in and out of the physical universe at the same time. You live within the physical universe, but it does not control you and it does not limit you. Sure, it limits your physical body, but you are not your physical body. You reside within your physical body when you are in the physical universe, but you are not spiritually bound by your physical body.

Absolute Love is of this world, and is also part of One. It is Absolute Love which connects you with the greater non-physical universe. It is Absolute Love which enables you to see the inner nature of all. Absolute Love is greater than romantic love, parental love, or friendship love, but they are a part of it. If you can love all beings with the same intensity, depth, and totality as you do with your parental or romantic love, then you are in Absolute Love.

While you are living in this physical lifetime, for good or for bad, you will keep coming back to your physical life even after connecting with Absolute Love. As far as I have yet discovered, Absolute Love is not stable or permanent while in this physical plane. Or, at least I have not yet attained the state where it is stable and permanent. If I reach a permanent state of Nirvana, I will bring it to you, and attempt to help you attain it. Stay tuned.

Some believe that if we have not attained Absolute Love in this lifetime, we are destined to return again so that we have another chance. Others believe that if we have been unable to find Absolute Love in this lifetime, upon death we go to some other place, or just cease. Could it be that the eve of this life becomes the dawn of a new life? No one really knows. What is known by those who have found Absolute Love is that it does transcend physical life.

Thomas Aquinas wrote that at the burning bush when Moses asked God who he was, "God answered Moses, 'I am that I am,' because God does not signify any particular form, but rather being, itself." [11] God is at the depth of your being where there is no form; and any attempt to describe God, or put God into words, would materialize God, and it would no longer be the common Oneness of all things.

Jesus said, "Neither shall they say, Lo here! or, lo there! for, behold, the kingdom of God is within you." [12] Jesus meant that you cannot find God through the physical senses. You can develop another sense to intuitively connect yourself to the spirit already within you.

In that place, there are no dualities. There is no good and evil, happy and sad, smart and dumb. In fact, there are no words. It is beyond all of that. Here is a down-to-earth, real-life illustration of how a deeper, non-dualistic reality can allow you to see beyond the world of black and white, and right and wrong. Once, when my wife and I were on a beach vacation, I found myself halfway to the beach when I remembered that I had forgotten the hat which I was ordered by my doctor to wear to protect my head from the sun. I went back and forth in my mind asking whether it was worth going all the way back to get the hat. Yes, or no?

My wife then reminded me that it was a cloudy day, and no sun to worry about. She had cut through the debate between yes and no to a deeper, more profound, realization. When you gain greater insight into the nature of all things, including yourself, you will find that you had been creating issues, dualities, and problems in your life where they need not exist. You may also come to realize that you have been unnecessarily, automatically, and subconsciously reacting to events, or people, and that such reactions have made you unhappy.

The Nature of Sin

From where do your knee-jerk emotional reactions and impulses come? Over your lifetime, or perhaps over sequential lifetimes, your ego has developed defenses, or rather primal reactions to things. They automatically kick in, even when unnecessary or self-destructive. When your genes were in a primal time, those fight or flight reactions were in the interest of self-preservation. They are now very rarely needed; and in fact, are usually counterproductive now that you are a highly developed, thinking human being.

In addition, as you grow up, you have both painful and happy experiences which shape your self-concept. They also shape your concept of others and the world. You build an image and a sense of self that overlays upon that pure being at your heart, and you come to identify with that self-image.

As a result, of pain experienced through life's events, your self-image, or ego, acquires feelings of insecurity, jealousy, fear, and other negative emotions; causing reactive behavior. Also, your life's positive experiences can cause you to have positive emotions such as self-confidence, faithfulness, and responsibility. If you are able to accept life's experiences with objectivity and wisdom, you will have the ability to better navigate life. You could even gain the ability to love and accept others in spite of their faults.

Those negative emotions or impulses try to take you over. You get "so angry!" Sometimes they can take over both your mind and your body. Anger is only one of them. You know them. Among them are fear, greed, jealousy, and insecurity. They can be an integral part of your ego.

Lust emanates from a desire to benefit yourself. It is greed. But greed leaves you endlessly dissatisfied. You never get enough through greed. You cannot find that which will make you truly happy. Love, on the other hand, creates a desire to give to another, to help another. To give, rather than to receive. Love makes you happy and content.

If you brag about your good deeds, people will see a braggart as well as the deeds. It lessens you in their eyes. Be modest. Let your deeds speak for themselves. If you bully, spread negative gossip, or denigrate others, it will reflect upon your character. The effects of those actions by you will cause people to see you as petty, spiteful, or mean. Their opinion of you will lessen, not of the person you are victimizing by your acts. If you are loving, kind, helpful, industrious, and work for the greater good, you need not worry about how people feel about you. You will know you are good and upright. You need nothing more. Do good for the sake of good. Not for egotistic prideful reasons. If you do good things solely in order to help your reputation or to get something in return, people will see through your actions.

Don't let your reactive mind take over just because it may be the first to chime in. Consider your actions before doing them. Even meditate upon them. Don't feel remorse for having succumbed to your lesser impulses. Instead, think about and correct them, and apologize.

If you give love and receive negativity in return from a person, it may be the lingering effects of some past actions of yours toward him or her. It is best to own your past negative actions by confronting them honestly, understanding them, and thus becoming able to sincerely explain them to the people you have hurt and truly seek forgiveness.

By acting out of anger, jealousy, or hatred you are showing that you are following a momentary satisfaction rather than your long-term benefit. Even in the short term, you have lived long enough to know that anger only begets anger in return. What good will that do you? Even looking at it in terms of your own self-interest, what benefits you more? Increasing an adversary's anger at you, or having them respect you?

If someone hates you, that is their problem. Don't make it your problem, too. Be honestly patient and friendly with everyone. You will be respected, even by those who wanted to oppose or hate you. Don't let the base, impulsive, animalistic part of you defeat your true good nature. Be true to yourself. Be happy and content, why not?

Don't act spontaneously from your reactions to people or events. Think about what your best reaction should be. Sleep on it, meditate upon it, and even consult others whose judgment you trust before acting.

If you have the urge to do something that you know will leave you with a negative emotion, don't do it. If it makes you feel shame or forces you to disregard feelings of shame, avoid it. Why intentionally walk into unhappiness?

Thrashing out and gaining revenge may seem easy in the moment, but it will hurt you in the long run, and in the deeper important run.

You will feel that instant reaction, but then you will remember the higher angel that you are. Remember what you have learned and take the high road. It is the road that will bring you happiness and contentment. Isn't happiness and contentment what you want?

We all make mistakes. If you make a mistake, acknowledge it. Express your regret to whomever it has hurt and do what you can to correct it and its results. There can be no embarrassment, selfishness, or egotism involved if you expect redemption from having done wrong. Being honest and strong is the only way to overcome a mistake. Believe me, others will sense you have done wrong. There will be an awkwardness and a hindrance to your relationships and your reputation until you end it by acknowledging your mistake and apologizing to whom you have hurt. Remember that lesson and do not repeat it. Then you will regain the respect of your friends, loved ones, and acquaintances. Overall, look deeply and objectively at your own actions. If you were wrong, admit it and learn from that mistake so you can do better the next time. If you do not admit your mistakes, how can you hope to do better?

Look at your mistakes honestly, and analyze them. Where did they come from? Teach yourself about them intellectually. Don't let the emotion prevent you from doing so. This is redemption. This is success. This is how you leave a legacy for your children and for the world.

If the harm to you is caused by fate, such as an illness, injury, or accident, it will do you no good to dwell long in bitterness. How will that change reality?

Certainly, you should use your human resourcefulness and intelligence to overcome that sickness or injury. But do not let it destroy you emotionally. Make the most of your transformed life. Don't let it interfere with your love of others.

The secret to success in life is not to be a genius but to learn to compensate for your weaknesses. Once you learn to accept your negative emotions and your weaknesses, you will be able to devise ways of compensating for them so that they no longer govern your actions.

Allow yourself to know you are okay and you will treat others better. You will no longer feel insecure or that you have something to prove, so you can be forgiving of others.

Marcus Aurelius, who was the emperor of the Roman Empire for two decades, learned much in his lifetime. In old age near his death he wrote his *Meditations* in the hope of passing on to others what he had learned. That included the following musing on ego and pride.

"...Is it your reputation that's bothering you? But look at how soon we're all forgotten. The abyss of endless time that swallows it all, the emptiness of all those applauding hands. The people who praise us – how capricious they are, how arbitrary. And the tiny region in which it all takes place. The whole earth a point in space – and most of it uninhabited." [13]

Want and desire are experiences of incompleteness. You succumb to greed, lust, anger, fear, jealousy, and other sins because you feel a lack within yourself. That something is missing in you. Finding your inner spirit will satisfy that need and leave you totally fulfilled. You are a free being. Don't let yourself be a slave to your negative feelings and impulses. Be free! You have the ability to rise above your negative feelings and urges. The power to do so is built into your godly human nature. You can cease being yanked around by the voice in your head.

Once you learn to accept your negative emotions and your weaknesses, you will allow yourself to treat others better. You will no longer feel your insecurities. You will no longer have something to prove, so you can be forgiving of others.

The Ego

Ralph Waldo Emerson in his lecture to the students of Harvard Divinity School in 1838 said: "The man who renounces himself comes to himself." Overcoming your ego is necessary to discovering the Oneness within you. That is because your ego makes you arrogant, selfish, jealous, shameful, or lustful. You cannot love while feeling those emotions.

Your ego has helped you progress through life on Earth, but it is a veil surrounding you which prevents you from seeing clear wisdom, or true reality. Clear wisdom, or absolute understanding is not a complicated philosophical theory. It is merely being able to see clearly what is in front of you. Once you are able to see through your egoistic veil to the true Oneness within you, your actions will create positive results, making you happy, successful, and well-liked.

By letting yourself feel hatred, jealousy, anger, envy, and the others, you are cutting yourself off from other people and from The One. Rejoin humanity, rejoin love, rejoin the best of what you are. Be the real complete you. Listen to your real nature–your spiritual light. That light is your connection to the spirit of all. That is your path to mutual love and respect with all of your brothers and sisters.

You are not meant to bounce from happiness to unhappiness and back again, extreme to extreme. You are meant to find balance within yourself, to be at peace so that you can avoid those primal knee-jerk reactions and feel and remember the love at your source. The love at your source is where you will find your umbilical cord to The One. Where you are simply there, simply a pure being. Where you also can say, "I am that I am," and simply be.

Some of your fears are helpful. Being afraid when you are on the edge of a tall cliff or reacting quickly when hearing a growl in the bushes are helpful. But, for example, if you are afraid to admit to even yourself that you are wrong about anything, the fear is counterproductive.

Usually, you are so controlled by those fears that they have become a subconscious part of your ego. You don't think about them, or even realize they are occurring. You just instinctively have a subconscious reaction to certain circumstances. Those reactions get in the way of you living a happy and successful life.

For example, a truck drives by, and without even thinking about it, the sound triggers the label "truck" deep in your brain. Instantly a combination of conclusions about "truck" is already in you. Loud, big, dangerous, "watch out," etc. This is true about everything. You subconsciously, automatically, and instantly come up with a set of conclusions about everything – including yourself.

These conclusions, or labels, form a veil between you and the real truth about everything and everybody. You see the world through that veil. Instead of seeing a truck, you see your set of conclusions about a truck. To see all as it really is, you have to see through that veil in which you live. The secret is to recognize when the veil is controlling you and to observe it objectively. The more you observe it objectively, the less control it will have over you. Once you see it for what it is, you can rise above it. After all, could it be that those counter-productive emotional patterns keep continuing because you keep reacting the same way without seeing through your veil?

If you feel the true spirit within you, you will observe the veil objectively, knowing it is not you. That will enable you to see beyond it, and to live your life's purpose. You will learn to shake your head and smile at yourself when you feel an initial primal reaction coming on, and not let it control you. You will then connect with the spirit of goodness you feel within you that raises you up and fills you with happiness. Isn't that a better way to go through life?

Would you rather keep zigzagging from one compulsion to another big and small, or start operating out of rational and loving wisdom? Isn't it about time that you became the master of your destiny? Became self-empowered? Fulfilled your purpose in life?

Once you learn to see behind your veil, you will realize that the presence of those very weaknesses that are within you are there in order to be overcome. They are meant to be. Haven't you already learned that major life lessons are learned through adversity? That is one of the important lessons of your Earthly life.

As you progress along your spiritual path, the veil will be lifted from your eyes and you will see your true potential. You will see those things you dismissed as not being worthy of your focus, actually are of the utmost value. Unbeknownst to you, they were the foundation upon which you have been building your life and developing your sense of what is important.

Once that veil has been lifted you will not regret that earlier you were unable to sense the eternal nature of your soul. You will then understand the hidden purposes behind it all. You will see that you cannot know light without having known darkness. You will eventually come to know that they are two aspects of the same thing and you will appreciate them both.

Perhaps the revelation you receive through the act of overcoming a character flaw will be the revelation which opens you to your Oneness, or at least gives you an incite which moves you to your next step upon your path. Those negative knee-jerk emotional reactions come from the karma in which the Hindus believe. Overcoming that karma can help you become One with the universe. Those initial knee-jerk reactions will stay within you. They are a part of you, but you do not have to be ruled by them. See them and objectively observe them. You can neutralize them. You can take the bite out of them. That will allow you to move past them. You can stop them from preventing you from achieving your life's goals and happiness.

If you get hung up on some urge to react in the moment to an event, one effective technique to overcome that momentary urge is to take a deep breath, or to "sleep on it," so you have time to consider the long-term consequences of that reaction. In the end what is important? What is for the best? The Zen practice teaches that there is wisdom in waiting.

Altogether those positive and negative subconscious instinctual emotions make you what you believe you are. They make up your ego, your self-concept. But you will come to realize that they are not really you. They are only as real as you make them. The only true reality is the reality of the present moment. Memories of past events are faulty, and the future is not yet determined. Once you see the true reality, your dealings with the ups and downs of life will be much easier. You will see them for what they are, and they will be unable to control you.

Your ego, the amalgamation of your inherited traits, your memory, and your feelings toward past events, is not the true realty. The only thing that is real is the present, and how you deal with it. Your ego buffets you about, and prevents you from being happy and doing goodness throughout your life. You should instead see clearly and be in the present moment as you travel through life.

If you have had children, you know that each child is born very different from the others. From the moment of birth, each is born with his or her own inborn unique way of dealing with life. Each is a spirit with an ego – trying to adjust to a physical life. That particular personal way of dealing with life is a permanent, yet evolving, part of every person. It interacts with each person's life experiences to further develop each person's individual ego or self-concept.

Where does that inborn attitude toward the world come from? The Hindu and Buddhist beliefs hold that we are destined to live successive lives. They believe that when our body dies, our soul, along with the sub-conscious experiences of all our successive lives, comes back to the Earthly plane in the body of a new baby of some sort. They believe that you are destined to come back to life in a new body over and over again until you have learned to connect to that pure spirit within you that is beyond mundane Earthly existence. They believe that once you have done so, you can then choose to go back and forth between Universal Consciousness and Earthly existence. But that when you are in Earthly existence, you will then be able to accept experiences without being controlled by your Earthly emotions and compulsions.

That belief in reincarnation was formed thousands of years ago before the study of genetics. It was a way to explain why babies have unique individual personalities from birth, as well as a way to inspire people to godliness or goodness. How is that different from coming back to life over and over again as a genetic string within a new baby? Isn't that what is happening according to modern science?

The genes keep becoming modified life after life in an evolutionary stream.

The science of epigenetics has now found that knee-jerk reactions can be passed on to offspring through the substance in the cell which surrounds the genes, the "epigenetic substance." The epigenetic substance activates or enhances some genes and turns off, or suppresses others. Therefore, even though you may have a gene carrying a destructive tendency, it need not be activated. The epigenetic substance surrounding that gene determines if that gene will be activated or not. Experiments have shown that traumatic events which occur in one lifetime of an animal can cause reactions in its children, even if only an insignificant aspect of it, such as a smell or a sound similar to the original event, has re-occurred. [14]

Each person has a unique genetic string. That string is surrounded by an epigenetic substance that determines from the moment of birth how that person approaches life on Earth. When that person has children, the genetic and epigenetic tendencies of the mother and father come together with all the amendments learned through millennia of historical experience and form another person with its own genetic and epigenetic tendencies. A person has a combination of those from the mother and father, both dominant and recessive. Your genes and epigenetic material make you more or less sensitive to certain positive or negative events. If you lack the corresponding negative memory within your epigenetic substance, you are likely to approach one kind of negative event with relative objectivity and wisdom. However, if you have the corresponding negative memory within your epigenetic substance, you will react to an event with primal emotion.

We all have them. Certain epigenetic memories are present in some people, but not in others. That is why some people react to some negative stimuli but other people do not. Epigenetic memories, and the reactions they cause, are part of your ego.

Even though you are governed to a certain extent by your genetic and epigenetic tendencies, you have individual self-destiny as well.

Through love, you can release yourself from the control of primitive emotional reactions, and learn to determine how to react to life's experiences. For example, two siblings grow up in the same abusive family and both are abused. One grows up to be an abuser. He or she has apparently learned that this is the way one gives and receives love in a family. This is a common negative cycle well known to mental health professionals and criminologists.

The extreme trauma of that person's upbringing causes him or her to react uncontrollably in circumstances which evoke the same emotions felt during the original trauma. The emotion is so strong that it overwhelms reason and conscience. It just blocks them out. This can be magnified from generation to generation as parents with certain genetic and epigenetic tendencies commit acts upon their children because of those inbred codes, which then create enhanced reactions in their children who have inherited those very same genetic and epigenetic tendencies. Hence, "the sins of the fathers are visited upon the children ..." [15]

Meanwhile, the other sibling from the abusive family has a slightly different mix of genes and epigenetic tendencies. Perhaps he has a soul which has learned to overcome certain tendencies. He grows up and deals differently with the abuse. While he is being abused, all he can think about is that he would never do this to another person. He knows what it is like to be abused. He knows how it feels, and would not wish it upon another. He becomes sensitive to the feelings of others and avoids causing harm. Causing harm to others makes him unhappy, just as he was unhappy when he was harmed. His empathy for others has been allowed to flourish due to his lack of a negative emotional reaction.

As a result, two siblings have the same experiences, but because of different mixes of inherited tendencies and life history, each deal with those experiences in very different ways. One way brings happiness, while the other brings misery.

There are other examples: Perhaps you were left by someone with whom you were deeply in love, and now you may avoid commitment and run away from relationships as soon as there is some problem. Or perhaps your father was always critical of you, and you could never please him. Now you feel inadequate and are riddled with self-doubt. Likewise, if you consistently received help and affection from your parents without judgment, you will be more likely to be trusting of others and able to give and receive affection without abnormally craving it. Whereas if you consistently received disapproval and disappointment from your parents, you are more likely to have an unusual need to receive approval and may do extreme or irrational things to get love and approval.

If you had been abandoned by your mother, you may be more prone to jealousy because you are worried about losing someone's love and affection. If you grew up with parents who heavily punished or abused you, you may later be constantly waiting to be hurt in a relationship. You may identify love with being hurt by a loved one.

If you were left to fend for yourself when you were young and thereafter became self-reliant, you may find it hard to connect with the suffering of others. You don't understand that others are not self-reliant like you. You have less empathy for them and do not understand why they are not self-sufficient.

The emotional pain may have hurt you so badly that you have resolved subconsciously to avoid it at all costs, using a primitive reaction. It may have implanted itself in your psyche, sometimes rearing its ugly head and overpowering you. Hurting you. Preventing you from achieving your goals, and accepting happiness.

Once you realize that your love comes from within you, it is always there and complete. Once you learn to love yourself completely, you will learn that you do not have to seek love or approval from others in order to be a whole, content person. You do not have to fear losing love from a particular person. The love within you will always be there, and you will know that giving love will cause you to get love.

If you are a victim of your experiences, and controlled by your knee-jerk reactions to them, you will be in a continuous cycle of unhappiness. Unhappy to you and unhappy to everyone around you. Can this cycle be stopped? Transcendental meditation and psychotherapy help. They have similar goals: knowledge of self. However, there are differences in technique, direction, and depth.

Psychologists believe the strategy is to go over the trauma again and again in your mind, living it over and over. They help you to investigate and revisit past experiences in order to better understand them intellectually. That process can neutralize the emotional sting, and thereby overcome the uncontrollable, subconscious negative emotions that come from them, and hurt your life. The goal is to remove a series of reactive emotions one at a time. Thus, understanding each better each time until each's bite is neutralized.

Transcendental meditation stills your ego, so that you see beyond it to your inner spirit. You receive insight and understanding of the inner nature of all things, including your ego. In that state you see the true nature of all emotional reactions in general, thereby helping free you from their control and the emotions they thrust upon you. That eventually allows you to be your true, egoless self.

Whereas psychotherapy can cause improvement along the horizontal plane of understanding one emotion, then another; transcendental meditation cuts deeply and vertically downward allowing you to see to the true inner reality of emotion itself. Once the inner nature of an emotion is understood, its hold upon you is diminished and can eventually disappear.

Meditating upon such emotions can help you see that there is now no need to react, or feel a certain way. You can come to finally understand each emotion with such depth of understanding that you see the perceived problem which originally caused the emotion no longer exists. You can see that the negative emotion that repeatedly overcomes you is not called for, because it is not from a current event. It is really you subconsciously reliving a deeply hurtful emotion you felt earlier in life.

Escaping from the control of your ego, and knowing what makes you unhappy, gives you the knowledge to make yourself and others happy. You will have learned what not to do. You will empathize with the pain within the other person, and you will feel it as well. That is the love connection between you and other people which allows both you and them to be happy.

Which makes you happy? Being steeped in negative emotion, or treating yourself and others with love? If you know what makes you and others unhappy, you have the knowledge and power to make you and others happy. Why not be happy? Why not be successful? Why not love and be loved? Why not be respected rather than be reviled? Why not be loved, rather than hated, or feared?

You can determine your direction in life. You can learn from your injuries how not to treat other people. After all, you know how it feels. You can live a positive, happy life helping others, thereby creating a positive cycle rippling throughout humanity and bringing you and others closer to the unifying One. That positive ripple's travels will be your gift to the world. Through that ripple, you will live forever.

It is not important, and probably impossible, to know exactly how your approach to life has been ingrained within you at birth. It is more important to rise above the ups and downs of life, so that you can traverse your life making yourself and others happy, and knowing and achieving your life's purpose. You cannot prevent unhappy or tragic experiences from happening in life, but you can learn to handle them calmly and rationally and learn from them. You cannot prevent storms from appearing on the sea's horizon, but each time you enter a storm you learn better how to trim your sails so as to minimize any future damage from them.

You will learn that your universal consciousness is your true self, and it exists behind your ego. You have the power to listen to your true self and apply what you learn to your life. You will thus gain the insight to choose to not succumb to reactive impulses. You also have the power to determine your future and reach your potential. The effects of life upon you are really the results of your relationship with your world. It is not what has happened, but how you have perceived it and dealt with it.

It has been seen throughout history that through losing their individualistic self, people have been able to rise above their miseries and live their full, happy potential. Through that process, you gain the wisdom and happiness of the unity of life. The infusion of The One within your worldly life gives you contentment and confidence. Your inner spirit has always been there waiting for you to arrive.

Through this teaching, I hope to help you gain the insight to look at a negative emotion objectively when it appears within you. You will see it objectively for what it is. You may remark to yourself about its persistence, maybe even laugh at it—"There I go again." Then you will connect to the love within you, and act through that love.

You will consider, with love, which direction makes you happy. You will therefore go toward happiness. Go toward love. Go toward friendship. What on Earth do you have to lose? Unhappiness?

You exist as part of the One Spirit. To hurt other parts of The One is to hurt yourself.

You will recognize it when you are within the Oneness. When you are within it, it is more real than anything you have ever experienced. Life and truth become so obvious. There is no doubt. Your life and the world around you are clarified and fully understood. With it comes a feeling of completeness, awareness, acceptance, and happiness.

You will realize that you are a part of all living things. You are not separate. If you think about it, all of our problems stem from our belief that we are separate from one another. If we were not separate, how could we be jealous, angry, lustful, or insecure?

You will never see the world the same again. Even when you are back living your Earthly existence you will remember enough of that experience to be a changed person. You will be profoundly changed by having "seen the light"-- The One. You will interact with the world in a different way.

You will have fewer lapses when the stress of the moment wants you to instinctively lash out, become jealous, angry, or perform some other "sin." You will not be so quick to judge others. You will have gained the power to control your instinctual reactions, rather than allow them to control you. You will be better able to navigate life.

Now, let us learn how.

HOW TO FIND THE ONENESS WITHIN YOURSELF?

The Limits of the Thinking Mind

You may not have previously been able to find The One, because you were thinking about it, rather than experiencing it. Your intellectual mind only knows things by their length, width, color, odor, sound, shape, taste, temperature, or consistency.

God has none of those qualities. Neither does love. Therefore, you cannot use thinking to truly experience it. As a matter of fact, trying to think about it will separate you from it. Remember what Jesus, an enlightened person, said: "The kingdom of God cometh not with observation. Neither shall they say, Lo here! Or lo there." [1] In other words, you cannot use your physical senses to find enlightenment. You can look here or there with your eyes, but you will not find enlightenment, which he called the Kingdom of God. He also said: "My kingdom is not of this world." [2] You, therefore, cannot find it through intellectual pursuits. It is beyond the physical world. It cannot be fully described in words to a person who has not experienced it. But once a person has experienced it, words are unnecessary.

Use love, inspiration, openness, sensitivity, and a focus on your own being in order to discover that spiritual power at the depth of your soul. It is that level of your existence which is more fundamental than your ego, and of any person's individual differences. It is the existence within you that is common to the existence within all other beings. It connects you with all other beings. It allows you to put yourself in their place, and still love them in spite of them doing things of which you disapprove, or do not understand.

That connection is outside of, and exists independent of your thinking mind. It is not dependent upon your thoughts, beliefs, and memories. It is not the product of your thinking mind. It cannot be perceived using your thoughts and your memories. The story of Adam and Eve's banishment from the Garden of Eden is a metaphor for the inability of the thinking mind to conceive of God. Adam and Eve knew God in the Garden of Eden, itself a metaphor for heaven, but when they began to use their thinking brain, i. e. when they acquired the knowledge of good and evil, they lost the ecstatic state of pure being within which they were able to sense the unifying force many call God.

That myth was preserved by the enlightened people who codified the Bible in order to teach that the knowledge of God cannot be found in the dualistic phenomenalistic world where there exists both good and evil; the world of the intellectual mind which thinks it is a body.

Furthermore, in Exodus 16:10, it is emphasized that God cannot be envisioned in the physical sense. In that story, it is said that "the glory of God appeared in the cloud." Also, in Exodus 10:18, it is said: "And Mount Sinai was altogether in a smoke..." The people were not able to use their usual physical senses to experience God. This phenomena and similar ones throughout the Old Testament, emphasize that you cannot experience God with your eyes, ears, touch, or smell. It takes the cultivation of another more subtle sense.

The Taoists say that "The Tao that can be perceived is not the Tao." The perception to which they refer is through the thinking brain.

The Buddhists call it the "Gate of No Thinking." When you pass through that gate, you enter what they call "The Path." Helping you find The Path, and keeping you on it, is the goal of this book.

It is independent of time and space. It is independent of the prejudices, fears, and desires you have developed in your lifetime on

Earth. It allows you to observe yourself; and objectively observe your prejudices, fears, and desires without being controlled by them.

All beings have a connection to The One, no matter their own path. It is The Path at the center of all paths. It is that which is common to all paths. It is the Unity, the commonality, The One. It is the calm within the storm; the place where you are content, because you understand all. It is the doorway to heaven. It is not every little thing, but the underlying force from which all things are created. It is the water from which each wave is created. So, you must quiet your thinking brain and be sensitive to your subtle, yet profound, spiritual interior. Remember the relationship of the wave to water. Water is the origin of the wave. "There are many types of waves, but water is homogeneous. Waves form and vanish, but water is eternal and inde-structible, and it remains so even when it appears and disappears." You must recognize that you are not really the wave. See through it to your true nature as the water.

Each of us must discover the Oneness within us in our own way, through our own inner path. You are on the right path if your path leads toward the Oneness, not away from it. That is if it brings people together, not apart. Helps rather than hurts, and joins rather than separates. Leads toward love; not hate, jealousy, fear, or retribution.

The path is not something external that you traverse. It is a journey within yourself to your origin; where you will find your true self. Traveling along your path puts you in natural harmony with pure Absolute Being. God is not manifested through worldly power but by internal awareness.

"To know that what is impenetrable to us really exists, mani-festing itself as the highest wisdom and the most radiant beauty which our dull faculties can comprehend only in their most primitive forms – this knowledge, this feeling is at the center of true reli-giousness." [3]

Whether you believe in one god or many gods, in an external god or internal spirit, in tradition and doctrine or internal discovery, you will eventually discover that all of those beliefs have love at their source. Love is transcendent. Love is the beginning, and love is the end. Love is at the core of all true spiritual, humanistic, religious, and even atheistic beliefs.

Finding Your Own Path

Different religious traditions emphasize different paths. Some of them put emphasis on strictly following the words written in their seminal texts as the immutable and holy word of their all-knowing god. Others emphasize living the ethical life as the means to go to heaven. While still others emphasize spiritual growth as to arrive at salvation through intuitive experience.

Each of us is wired differently. Some people see the world through fundamental black-and-white terms and benefit through strictly following rules and instructions. Perhaps the Earthly wisdom path is better for practical and intellectually-oriented people who value ethical behavior and find God through doing unto others as they would want to be done to them. Meanwhile, intuitive aesthetically-oriented people may lean toward spiritual experience leading to revelation. My observation is that some people are born with a mixture of those tendencies, but many others lean toward one definite path or another.

Each person has to find the path that clicks with him or her. So long as one's heart is in the right place, the best paths or techniques are those to which each person is naturally drawn and which "makes the most sense" or "feels right." Every person can find his or her own path to the top of the mountain. The aboriginal praying to the spirit within the lake, the Abrahamic faithful praying to their external God, and the spiritualists and mystics who quiet their minds and touch their inner spirit all begin on different paths determined by the state of their soul. But all those paths lead eventually to the same place. We all may be on different paths, and on different places along our paths. We may have different understandings and rituals appropriate to our times and places, but if love is at the source of our practices and beliefs, we are on the right path–The Path.

You can touch heaven no matter your level of intellect, worldly sophistication, or spiritual understanding. The awareness emanating from the Oneness within me tells me that every person, no matter his or her personality, or way of dealing with the world, is able to connect with his or her spiritual path to The One–to absolute love–in his or her own way, through his or her own personal path. Some paths may not be as spiritually oriented as others at their beginning. But why should they be thought of as less valid? Both those people who live their day-to-day lives according to religious teachings and those others seeking spiritual awareness will regularly make mistakes and temporarily lose their way. Progress is made by those who learn from their mistakes and apply that learning to their movement along their own chosen path, whatever it is. The great traditions recognize that spiritual awareness is not complete unless it is practiced in the world.

So, my goal in this book is to help you find that personal connection within you which will become your doorway to heaven. It should not matter what your path is. I want the broadest spectrum of my readers to be able to put my teaching to successful use. How valuable could this be if only those already on the path to enlightenment can gain from it? And what is the real value of the Oneness to us if it is unavailable to some of us? It is within the power of all people to travel within themselves to the pure spirit within them. Every person has the spark of divinity within them. To follow your light is the path to the unifying force connecting all.

Maharishi Mahesh Yogi teaches very different types of souls, each having its own path to the transcendent. He speaks of the person who thinks in terms of the intellectual, whose path involves intellectually progressing from experiences of a gross nature to experiences of a more subtle nature, and finally reaching the particular experience of the transcendental state. He speaks of the emotional person who approaches God by progressing through the ever deeper and ever wider feelings of love, until reaching the love of all and becoming One. He speaks of the physically-oriented person whose regular practice of meditation causes his nervous system to experience more and more previously undetected subtle senses until it gains the full awareness of pure consciousness. He describes the psychologically-oriented person, who through regular meditation, follows a path offering greater ease and more rapid realization of truth until it reaches the state of transcendental consciousness. There is also the person who has always focused his or her life upon physical activity, who can through the practice of regular meditation learn to direct his or her activity from the outwardly physical to the inner direction, creating a state of stillness and restful alertness which allows for the perception of absolute consciousness and enlightenment. He tells of how each may be taught to find that transcendent spirit within themselves through meditation, the practice of mindfulness, to connect with their inner spirit. [4] Meditation has been proven over many centuries to work, and it has been used successfully by people of all religions, and of no religion.

There are many scriptures that can lead you to the eternal One, not just one. By holding up one of them as the only one, you are totally missing the point. Every person is different and therefore he or she should find the path to God which touches a chord within them. Also, you will find that as you progress along your path to spiritual awareness, you will connect to your path in different ways, each corresponding to that certain place along the path in which you then find yourself. Different types of connections to your unfolding soul will present themselves to you when you are ready to hear and see them. They had always been there, but you then will be ready to gain insight from them.

If you insist on holding onto old perceptions, thereby closing your heart to new revelations, you will not progress toward enlightenment. Just because something connected with you at an earlier stage of your life does not mean you should not be open to others as you progress, so that you can gain new insight. If you feel that you have lost connection with your religious experience and it has gone stale, you should allow yourself to be open to new revelations as they appear before you.

Go one step at a time. Take what you are ready for. It is movement. You will be on The Path. Discover it. Meander within it. Your path will be winding and will contain stagnant pools, as does a river along its path, but it travels on as do you. Find the spirit of Oneness within where you are in life. If you find the spirit at the root of a certain place, you will naturally know the next step. One builds upon the previous. Don't worry about achieving enlightenment right away. Let it be, and it will eventually come.

How do you know if you are on the path of Oneness, or if you have gone astray? You should ask yourself: "Am I loving the goodness within others? Am I helping others? Have I been treating every other person with brotherly love? Do I understand down deep that we are all in this together, and that in the end, we all seek the same thing? As I walk down the pathways of life, do I cast goodness and light around me like ripples upon the water, spreading and touching all around me and making the world better?" Marcus Aurelius in his *Meditations* put it this way: Do what "leads to fairness, and self-control, and courage, and free will." [5]

If you strive egotistically to be respected and loved for selfish reasons, it doesn't really happen. People see through it. Haven't you learned that yet? And have you yet learned that when you do things for personal gain, you just do not achieve the heights that you do when you act for a greater purpose? What a paradox! When your ego sets out to be respected and loved, people see through it and you do not really receive respect and love. But if you forget your ego, and act out of a higher purpose beyond yourself, people naturally respect you and are drawn to you.

When you feel the spirit within you, you are not afraid of other people, or afraid to interact with them. You are open to ideas that conflict with your assumptions. You know that your assumptions are the product of your imperfect memory interacting with your ego.

Karen Armstrong, the religious historian, says that earlier in life, because she did not accept the orthodox doctrines of religions, she considered herself an atheist, or agnostic. That was before she started her research for her landmark book, *A History of God*. Through her research for that book, she found that all religions encourage one to become free from one's ego in order to receive the transcendental experience which is called, among other things, God. She says that she now finds her spiritual meaning through loving her fellow man.[6]

Why not love your fellow man and do good by them? How can that be wrong? By doing good and helping people you will also feel happiness, contentment, and life fulfillment; and may even periodically receive profound revelations or insights.

Can you live on The Path without consciously following a religious or spiritual tradition? Sure. Humanists can be some of the most generous, kind, and forgiving people on Earth. They act out of the goodness of their hearts. They live a life connected to The One. It is not necessary to intellectually recognize The One within you. So long as you live it, it is there. When you finally fully understand yourself, your self will become immaterial, unimportant.

What's more, if you love your fellow man and dedicate your life to helping people or society, why aren't you acting out of universal consciousness, or God, even if you don't consciously realize it? And does it matter that you don't consciously realize it if you are living it? Remember, you cannot understand it by rational thought, and trying to categorize or name it is counterproductive.

Confucius believed that The Path's destination is not a place such as a heavenly city. He wrote that the destination of The Path is a condition. A "tranquil state that comes from appreciating that it is the following of the way itself that is of ultimate and absolute value." [7]

Confucius in <u>Analects</u> 9:4 also said, "The nobleman is the man who most perfectly having given up self, ego, obstinacy and personal pride follows not profit but the Way. Such a man has come to fruition as a person; he is the Consummate Man. He is a Holy Vessel."

Through the practice of meditation, you can recognize where you are at this moment in the spiritual progress of your soul, and then you can shape it to overcome your weaknesses and psychological road-blocks so as to have your soul take quantum leaps toward your enlightenment. That is within your power.

You are already on your life journey. Do you want to travel consciously or unconsciously? With your eyes open, or your eyes closed?

Karen Armstrong wrote in *The Spiral Staircase*: "The religious traditions were in unanimous agreement. The one and only test was that it must lead directly to practical compassion" [8] and that "editing out our ego is –- I now realize – an essential prerequisite for religious experience." [9] Acting out of love, out of a dedication to a thing greater than yourself, being inspired to help others– who can say that is not God, your ultimate Oneness, acting through you?'

Judaism teaches that the highest form of godliness is putting it to work to help others. If you spend your life acting from that inspiration, it does not matter whether or not you call it "God." No label is necessary. It is what it is. Remember: "I am that I am."

Meditation

There is a disagreement among some religious scholars. Some believe that spiritual enlightenment, the internal light of God, comes through a sudden mystical revelation such as they say came to Mohammed and the Jewish prophets – a "calling." There are others who believe that the ability to experience that inner, illuminating spirit comes through the patient drifting away from the busy world, which is achieved through contemplation and meditation. Both are correct.

You do not know when your enlightening revelation will come. Moses, Jesus, and Mohammed's sudden unexpected revelation occurred while they had been spending long, solitary periods on a mountain, wandering in the desert, or in a cave. All in all, away from the world. Jacob's mystical experience of God occurred while he was utterly alone in the desert, contemplating his banishment from his family, and trying to sleep with a rock for his pillow.

Mohammed said: "The spirit comes at the bidding of my Lord, and ye are given but a little knowledge thereof." [10] You cannot predict when your revelations will come. Mine occurred in the middle of the night after I had been staying awake for a long period of time studying, thinking, and contemplating. I did not realize it, but that was a form of meditation. It frequently has happened that way. A revelation comes to a person while he or she is separated from normal daily life, on a mountain, in the desert, or in a cold room all by himself with the outside world shut out. Callings, revelations, or epiphanies, through which people see the true nature of life, are more likely to come during such periods of meditation.

I cannot know if Jacob, Moses, or Mohammed had inklings of the Oneness before their big revelations, but as I explained in the introduction to this work, I did. At the age of seven or eight, and again at about twelve, I had similar revelations with the same conclusion; that I and my tormentors were the same down deep; that I should not hate them, but understand them and empathize with them. During those times I did not think it was "God" that I was realizing, but the Oneness among beings.

In November 1969, in the midst of swaying to music, I had my first ecstatic spiritual experience. The music was uplifting, and I felt the feeling of Oneness from the happiness and unity of purpose and multitude within which I found myself. Again, the realization was not of "God," but of a profound unity with others, and a profound optimism that the problems of the world could be transcended.

It was not until the message of love during the Christmas season which filled my heart, that I made the profound connection. The message of Jesus was that of love and unity with all mankind, and I suddenly realized that message was the answer to all! I later came to see that same message within Judaism, Islam, Buddhism, and other religious and non-religious teachings.

It didn't come to me as an intellectual conclusion. It came to me as a spiritual revelation, an epiphany. A burst of understanding that was beyond words and thinking. It was a recognition of a life apart from the normal world, but somehow permeating throughout it.

I danced through life for months with that revelation. I could think or speak of little else. I was like a blossoming flower. I was ready. I was open. In the next year, I allowed into my consciousness people and events which I otherwise may have passed by without notice. They had profound effects on me. They expanded my realization of myself and the nature of life.

"I am not my body!" I remember the moment that realization came to me. "I am a spirit which inhabits this body. This body is merely my vehicle in this Earthly world, but I can be beyond this body, beyond my physical senses. I exist beyond the physical world! My existence, my awareness, my understanding, is not limited by the physical, the intellectual, the mundane, the Earthly!"

Looking back and remembering that event, I now realize that it was a meditative experience leading toward a revelation. We sat still for a long time, not moving a muscle or even our eyes; and we were taught to be unaffected by the disruptive experiences thrown at us. Our bodies were unmoved and our eyes were fixated upon a spot in front of us, but our spirit was very much free and alive. In order to accomplish the act of being above and beyond what was happening around me, I allowed my consciousness to enter a state beyond normal consciousness.

Then came the sessions in Tyrone's living room. Each day after the sessions ended, I spent hours letting the spiritual feeling wash over me and through me. I often sat on my mattress after a session and listened over and over again to the song, "My Sweet Lord," on George Harrison's album, "All Things Must Pass." It drew me closer to The One. You should try that when you are meditating. You will see what I mean.

I did not know what meditation was at that time, but I was doing it. Those times were contemplative, ascendant, and luminous. They were not of this mundane world. I personally only know my own experience, but enlightenment masters have written that through the intense open awareness achieved through the regular practice of meditation, the mind-blowing, yet calm and blissful awareness of spiritual enlightenment eventually comes with natural inevitability.

Within spiritual enlightenment, your consciousness is expanded beyond the limits of your body's mind, into infinity. In order to find and follow your spiritual path, you must release yourself from the control of your ego. That is done through regular devoted meditation. But always remember that meditation is the means. It is not the end. It leads to mindfulness, which allows your spiritual consciousness to develop.

So, the lesson in this is that the people who believe that we receive God, the Oneness, the eternal universal spirit within us, through a sudden unexpected revelation, or "calling" are correct. And the people who believe that one can achieve such revelations through inner contemplation and meditation are also correct. Spiritual belief-shattering revelations come unexpectedly, but they are more likely to come at a time when you are not controlled by, or in the grasp of, mundane day-to-day life. This can happen at a time of great crisis when you come to question your fundamental assumptions and beliefs. It can also be brought on by a more predictable, controlled process of releasing yourself from your assumptions and beliefs and seeing beyond your ego to your true nature.

This can be done through the regular practice of meditation, which you can think of as a form of prayer. Through meditation you allow your ego to melt away, and you become receptive to your inner calm, clarity, awareness, and wisdom. It eventually leads you to the total universal understanding that was received by Moses, Muhammed, Buddha, Jesus, and so many others.

Your path toward Oneness will eventually diffuse into your way. I picture a "path" as having edges and boundaries. It is identifiable and separate. I picture a "way" as having diffuse boundaries and over-lapping with other ways, having parts in common with other ways. It can be shared with other beings. Being in The Path, and eventually The Way, is a reward unto itself. Seeing The One, even fleetingly, is life-changing. You will see your essential true nature for the first time. You will find your life's purpose.

You will know when you are there because you will have awakened. You will have connected with the source of all life. You will discover who you really are, and your true nature will become unveiled. Your busy physical world will thin out to only a film through which you will "see" your true self. You will become free from your ego, your flawed personality. You will let go of any concern for the objects of the world. You will have returned to that state of pure awareness which is the source of all individual life. Pure undifferentiated existence. The source of all life will reveal itself. You will become all-encompassing and all-knowing. You will be everything and everything will be you. From a limitless existence, you will be able to objectively observe the machinations of your limited self. You will simply be aware of your entire consciousness.

When within The One, I dissolved into infinity. Universal consciousness is a consciousness beyond the distinctions of subject and object, good and bad; beyond relativity.

Once you are on The Path, you will want to stay there. However, having to navigate in the work-a-day world will eventually take over your momentary living, and will push The Path into the background. In this book, I will explain to you how to make it more likely that you will experience The One, and how to then maintain a practice that will keep it in your consciousness. Maintaining such a practice will make you more receptive to receiving more and more insights and revelations, each bringing you closer and closer to spiritual enlightenment. It is through such revelatory experiences, that you will eventually attain spiritual enlightenment, that you will develop a lasting realization of the nature of existence.

Empathy and compassion are The Way. The Way is the place where you can truly walk a mile in everyone's shoes, and do unto them as you would have them do unto you. Once you connect with even your enemies at that level, and have a common understanding at that level, you can develop a bond with them that transcends the differences at the surface of you both. You will be happy, and you will be far more able to achieve your purpose in life. Remember that Abraham welcomed strangers into his tent, and they turned out to be messengers from God. That is a metaphor. Abraham recognized God even in the stranger. It was a test. In a deep sense, God or The One, is just as much within the stranger and the enemy, as it is within you and those close to you whom you know you love.

This does not mean that you will overlook their transgressions. To love all beings is not to let them hurt themselves or others. It is said that the child most difficult to love needs it the most. Your love for your children compels you to sometimes punish them or separate them from others for their own good or the good of others. As a parent supervising the play of young children, you do not become emotionally involved when one child bites or hits another child, or grabs a toy from a child and that child begins to cry. You are at a level of understanding above theirs. You handle the situation empathetically, objectively, and calmly; perhaps separating them, or sending a child to his room. In that same way, universal unconditional love does not prevent you from punishing people for bad acts, or from separating them from society in order to protect society, and teach them a necessary life lesson.

Nothing is perfect in this physical world. It is for us to see the perfection within the imperfection. Love is the way.

Finding Yourself in Others

Have you yet learned that your ability to connect with your fellow human beings is a great part of your success in life? So, how do you come together with another with whom you are in conflict? It is by finding the commonality, the unity between you. Begin by looking for how you and they are the same, even, if necessary, at the most basic level. Are you both parents or grandparents, both getting older, both misunderstood, both women, etc.? Start from there. Get to know them first as friends, then as people.

Your Earthly life is a place of learning and doing, and also a place of loving. Through your life, you are an instrument through which the harmony of life should be played. So work, play, and sing together with all other beings in joyful sharing of this wonderful, physical world into which we have all been placed.

Have empathy. Consider the innumerable people who have contributed to your being here today. We are all interconnected. No one is alone. There is a great commonality among people which cannot be avoided. In fact, it must be sought.

For example, think about your simple ability to eat a chicken salad sandwich. How many people have contributed their effort, skill, and heart to make it so you have it to eat? They include the farmer who raised the chicken, the canner, the wholesaler, and the person who owns the market where you bought it. It is the farmer who grew the celery for the packer, the distributor, and the marketer of that celery. It is the farmer who grew the wheat for the roll, the baker, and all those truckers. They all contributed to your sandwich. We are all in this together. You are never alone. Appreciate the network of life. Follow the common connection, the common contributions that make up life.

If you are a farmer or fisherman, revel in the life you bring to the world through the food you harvest. If you are a laborer, revel in what you are creating and how it improves the lives of others. If a weaver, revel in the joy and comfort your cloth brings. There can be love in all you do. And that love unifies you with all mankind. It unites you with The One. Your loving contributions to the world are just as valuable as the work of a surgeon or spiritual leader. It is important to love your work so that you can be true to yourself. If you have a choice, why voluntarily be unhappy in your work? Do what you love so that you can share in the joy of life, and perform your life's purpose. You have the power within you to find love and joy in the things you do.

Listen. When you are speaking, you are only repeating what you already know or believe. When you listen, you can learn something new. You can expand your consciousness and knowledge. You can gain further wisdom.

You never really know what the people around you may be going through, so treat them with kindness. There is good in everyone, even though they may have been affected by events that caused them to approach the world and its people in destructive ways. Down deep they are like you. They are looking for love. Look for the love in them. Feel it!

Stop the cycle of hate with love. Assume the best, and you may find the best. If you receive hatefulness or aggression, give love in return. "If we could read the secret history of our enemies, we should find in each man's life sorrow and suffering enough to disarm all hostility." Henry Wadsworth Longfellow [11]

Giving kindness or generosity is not just your act. Someone is simultaneously receiving your kindness or generosity, so they are acting as well. You are brought together by that act.

If you want to be happy, how easy is it for you to be happy in a room full of happy people, compared with trying to be happy while surrounded by a room full of unhappy people? And now look at it from the other direction. Think about how hard it would be for you to stay unhappy in a room full of happy people. You are not alone. You are truly connected to others whether you like it or not.

Be careful that you do not give for the wrong reasons. Helping someone can be a way of taking control, or giving can be done to enhance your ego. You should refrain from giving charity for self-interest, such as giving so as to expect something in return.

Doing the right thing, because you are taught that it is "the right thing to do" is admirable, because so many people have not even met that challenge. But doing the right thing because you understand that it is an act of love and promotes the bond of unity among all people is the ideal with which you should identify.

Every human being wants happiness. People who hurt you are not evil. They are merely unskilled at being happy. If you are unskilled at being happy, here are some skillful behaviors you can adopt to help yourself. Listen to the other person, care about others, be kind, and be patient with people. Even if a person does not appreciate your good intentions, treat them kindly even though you have an initial angry reaction within yourself. Don't let your reactive mind take over just because it may be the first to chime in. Consider your action before doing it. Take time to meditate on it. If you fail and succumb to your lesser impulses, do not let remorse overcome you. Instead, think about what you have done, correct it, and apologize.

If you give love and receive negative feeling in return from a person, it may be the lingering effects of some past actions of yours toward him or her. It is best to own your past negative actions by confronting them honestly, understanding them, and thus becoming able to sincerely explain them to the people you have hurt, and truly seek forgiveness.

Consider the substance of things rather than their mere appearance. That will bring you closer to the truth, and will better guide your thoughts and actions.

If you understand the source of both approval and of disapproval, you need not be controlled by either. If you know you are living your life rationally and kindly out of the love of others, you will not feel the egoistic drive that succumbs to either approval or disapproval.

Don't allow yourself to become fooled either by others or by yourself. Look frankly at whatever it is that you are doing, analyze it, and size it up with honest eyes. See its ramifications and effects – long, mid, and short-term. Does it make the world better? Is it empathetic and just? What harm does it cause? Does it fulfill or harm your spirit? Will it make you truly happy?

External events are not the problem. It is your perception of them that hurts you. You have power over your perceptions; your emotional reactions. Remember that the past is only faulty memory, and you cannot determine the future. Steady yourself, and consider from where your hurtful feeling originated. How important is it now? Looking back through hindsight, could things have been done differently? Did you react correctly? Could your perceptions have changed the outcome of that which so haunts you now? You can bring your life into control. You can overcome the memory of those traumatic past events that hinder your present happiness.

If you regret not acting when you should have, don't regret it. Act. Act as you should have. If you regret acting inappropriately from anger, jealousy, lust, greed, fear, or some other emotion that once controlled you, bury the regret by honestly apologizing and making it right. If you do truly regret it, you will not be embarrassed by doing so, and you will be relieved. You will be truly redeemed. You will become free of that pain. You will be able to learn from the experience so that it will not be relived, or repeated. You will have grown. Become wiser. Happier. Godlier. You will be further along your path to absolute understanding; to enlightenment.

Your imperfections will always be in you and will regularly try to rise, but what you have learned about loving others can always overcome them. You can make every event into one of goodness. You can see beauty and deliverance within the pain.

Go for the good, that which benefits others, not for adoration, approval, or personal benefit. Good, just, or beautiful things are inherently good, just, or beautiful.

If you receive love from others, you must love others. If you want kindness, you must give kindness out of love, and not because you want kindness in return. You should give kindness, love, respect, and generosity as the natural, automatic, result of the love you feel for all living things. The world will eventually treat you well if you treat it well. Let all you do and say be guided by your sense of unity with and love for all things.

Find a way to work for a world of brotherly love, a world of peace, of happiness. We are all in this together. When you give love, you get love. No matter what you find to do in this physical world, do it so as to spread universal love.

You say: "I could never work with that *@?#! person! He believes _____." Befriending and seeking common goals with that person achieves two things that you want. First, it fills your being with love and contentment, rather than hate. You become happy, not miserable. Secondly, it better achieves your own personal goals, because once you begin working with a person, you can work further with that person. Once you find some common goals, you will find others.

Two heads are better than one. If your eventual goals are the same or similar, how does it help the achievement of your own goal to denigrate or sabotage a different technique toward achieving that same goal? Work together side-by-side, or separately, but don't hurt your own interests by seeking the differences. Seek the commonalities, and reinforce them. If you work side by side with another toward a mutual or similar goal, you will be more effective than just working by yourself. Isn't that better than being angry, and throwing hot coals at each other? As my mother used to tell me when I was young: "You get more with honey than with vinegar."

Put yourself in the shoes of others. In the shoes of the angry, the evil, and the despised. Feel their pain, and work to end it.

If you harm even a small portion of mankind, you are harming the whole of mankind.

What benefits all of mankind cannot truly harm you in the end. Be flexible. Take what comes and make the most of it.

Work with others to try to find agreement on some things, or at least a respectful dialogue between fellow travelers on the road of life. You have different life experiences, so you may approach similar goals with different strategies. Maybe you can work together, or separately, to accomplish those shared goals. At the very least, you can respect each other's efforts.

Why must it be one way or the other? Your fundamental goals are similar, such as sharing happiness with family, and being free of worry. Why can't there be mutual respect, or even support, for your different ways of achieving them? This will accomplish more toward fulfilling your own goals, than will anger and conflict. Feeling compassion for others will also help you feel compassion for yourself. You and the other person are both trying to be happy; both trying to overcome your weaknesses, and the lingering effects of past wrongs.

You are both trying to support a family, or trying to get though school, or whatever it might be. Find a kinship with that person through a commonality.

How? Ask questions and keep a totally open mind. Don't use words with emotional baggage. It will divide you, and hinder your work for goodness. If you feel you disagree about something, analyze your various definitions of that thing. You may find that much, or all, of your differences, stem from you and them putting different definitions upon the same words. Speak of your differences in terms of what connects you. Ask yourself: "What are they seeing that I don't see?"

If they say, "I will never allow A." Ask "What do you mean by A?" Probe with an open receptive mind; not in an attempt to change their thinking, or to criticize them. You both may find that you have more agreement than disagreement. You both may find that there are exceptions to "never" to which you both agree. You may find that you have been merely disagreeing with each other's definitions, or drawing a line somewhat differently, but agreeing fundamentally. Maybe there is an overlap between your beliefs. Maybe you agree about 70 percent and disagree only about 30 percent.

Keep asking "why?" repeatedly with honest wonder and an open mind. Tell them that you truly want to understand why they believe as they do. You are asking so that you can learn. Keep asking until you are able to see the truth within their belief, and can experience it yourself. Approach a dialogue with another person with a mind eager to learn. Don't you want to keep learning? Isn't it interesting to learn new things? If you are not ready to consider a new viewpoint, you will stay at your current level of understanding, and not become wiser. Is that what you want?

Don't be afraid of change. You are always changing. You can't stop it. Approach new ideas with an open, eager mind. You have nothing to fear but fear itself. Be willing to be surprised. Hope to be surprised. Enjoy the adventure of learning new things. Don't you want to keep learning in life? Don't you want to grow as a person? Don't you remember how interesting it was to learn new things?

"It too shall pass." All things in this life are transitory. Change is always happening. Accept it. Live it. It is a truer reality than holding onto imperfect memories, or being controlled by unexamined beliefs. The world is unfolding and evolving. Do your best to give love within it while you are in it.

It is OK to rethink your assumptions. Hey, you may actually learn something.

Change is good. It means you are growing. It is an adventure. It is exciting. It is inevitable.

You may also say that you don't want change. It is comfortable to know what to expect. It is peaceful to follow the same routine day after day. But are you really happy? Are you really loved? Is your life comfortable, but uninspired? Are you succeeding at your life's purpose? Do you even know your life's purpose? Do you have a sense that there should be something more to life? Do you have some vague sense that you are really something other than what you pretend to be? Do you have a sense that something is missing from your life? Then maybe you still have more to learn. Do you remember when learning was fun? When life was an adventure?

You can know yourself and be comfortable when interacting with all people. You can have mutual respect with everyone. You can experience a state of being which has always been within you, but which you have not been able to experience through your thinking mind which has been at the mercy of your ego. You must allow yourself to separate from your ego; your old idea of who you think you are.

Certainty without love starts wars. Certainty without love allows people to bomb countless innocents. Certainty without love has allowed men to stone women of their own faith who try to pray with them.

But, at the same time, you must remember that there are some basic eternal parameters of conduct that were formulated by very wise people who were inspired by the Oneness they had discovered within themselves, the love within them. Among them: Do not kill. Do not steal. I think all good-hearted people can accept that these rules and others are at the boundaries of acceptable human behavior. To violate them requires a very important mandate.

Remember that the spirit of a law is more fundamental than the letter of the law, and that your goal is to seek balance rather than extremes. Think of the draftee in war and the starving person stealing bread to stay alive.

Disillusionment with life can leave you rudderless, depressed, and desperate. It is at a time such as that that you can receive an epiphany. You can see a truth that you had previously been unable to see because you were previously immersed in an accepted certainty. But be sure that such truth comes from love. Always be on the path of goodness and mercy. Do no harm. If you do good, you will stay on The Path to the Oneness of your spirit which connects you to all beings, and thus, to God. If you do good, you will be happy.

Feeling a kinship with the person with whom you are dealing makes you feel happier than if you feel that person is an enemy of some kind. Instead of making assertions, ask questions with an open mind in order to try to better understand each other's feelings. That will help each of you gain a deeper understanding of each other.

If there is greater understanding, there is more likely to be love and compassion. With less understanding, you are more likely to be harsh and narrow. To understand all is to forgive all.

Be kind to everyone, because everyone is involved in life's struggles just as you are. No one is perfect, and everyone is trying to be better and happier in their own ways, just as you are.

Try to remember that blaming a person for doing something hurtful is like blaming the stick used by a person to beat an animal. The stick is merely the instrumentality used by the person. It is useless to blame the stick. Likewise, that person is the instrumentality being used by the primal emotion within him or her. Blame that negative emotion rather than the person. Parents are similarly taught that when their child does something wrong, they should not tell their child that the child is bad. They should teach their child that the certain act they have performed is bad, and must be stopped. That allows the child to look at the act as something different than themself. Instead of giving the child a damaged self-esteem, and making the child defensive, the parent is allowing their child to see that they can separate themselves from that act. Hopefully, that child will eventually look at that act with objective eyes and reject it. If the parent tells the child that the child itself is bad, it will be much harder for that child to separate themself from that act.

Every person's way of approaching something is formed from their life experiences laid upon their genetics. There may have been misunderstandings of motives, misperceptions of past events, or just different ways of seeing the world. Restrain yourself from believing that yours is the only truth. Doesn't life experience show us that the truth is always somewhere in the middle? Do you think you have nothing left to learn?

Haven't you learned that memories are often faulty? Lawyers know that different witnesses to the same event often describe it in a courtroom in very different ways. Would you bet your life that your version of something which happened long ago is the only true one?

Love with Wisdom

Khalil Gibran, in his illuminating book, *The Prophet*, says that your passion is your sail and your reason is your rudder. [12] Your heart will show you the path, and your brain will remind you of the parameters. Love and wisdom; mercy and judgment; what a combination. You do need both.

Here is an example. Each day as you walk home from work or school, you pass a corner where a homeless, obviously destitute, person is begging for money. You regularly give the person change out of the goodness of your heart. But eventually, you notice that the person is constantly drunk. You now know that any money you give that person will be used to buy more liquor, and likely hasten their destruction. What do you do?

Use your life wisdom gained from experience to know that he may one day have the opportunity to find himself and become a happy, healthy, constructive human being. And use your love to have faith in him, and to decide to give him money to keep him alive another day. For on that day, he may gain the strength to change his life. Wisdom must interpret life's experiences from the standpoint of love, and not from pure intellect.

It is better if giving brings you joy, rather than regret. But the best reason for giving is that it is the natural expression of love within the parameters of wisdom. The difference between knowledge and wisdom is that knowledge is defined as coming from fixed ideas whereas wisdom allows you to be open to questions. Bear witness and observe everything from all viewpoints, and then you can take action in the world.

See the wonder of God in everything – in the sky, the sea, birds, trees, and even in your fellow humans. There really is nothing mysterious or difficult about it. It is the natural way of things. The spiritual force is already within you. It has been drowned out by the hassles of daily life, and the hurts you have endured. It is at your source. Listen to it. Let it blossom.

Don't get hung up on the whys of it. That will only draw you away from the Oneness. Focusing on the why of it will make you focus on the different paths rather than our common destination: the Oneness of all things.

Every person must enter their own Path in their own way. Later you will eventually find that there is so much overlap between your path and that of others that even a small bit of additional knowledge can put you both on a common path. Working together toward those common goals can only help you achieve your own.

There are many levels of understanding. Start where you feel comfortable. It will do no good to try to be at a level that doesn't fit where you are. Start where you are, and seek Oneness with others. Let what will be, be. Let it flow, and as it flows, open yourself to it.

Doubt is the beginning of wisdom. Be open to rethinking your mind's conclusions, and open up your heart. Let go of your mind's conclusion that you are separate from other people. Consider that your belief that you are in this by yourself is at the foundation of your feelings of jealousy, anger, betrayal, greed, and the other "sins." They couldn't exist if you didn't feel that you are separate from other people.

As we have learned, those negative emotions are not you. They are mere constructs of your mind. They only gain reality when you succumb to the assumptions of your ego.

Heaven and Hell

It may be that heaven and hell exist in every moment. If you live in the spirit of The One, doing unto others as you would have them do unto you out of love, you are feeling heaven. But when you are seething in hate, revenge, or jealousy, you are in hell. Think about it. You do not have to wait for a life after death or a great time of reckoning. You are how you live your life day to day. Remember: "I am that I am." The present is the only true reality. Live each moment out of love.

It makes no difference if there is reincarnation, Judgment Day, life after death, or a heaven and hell after you leave this Earth. Life is in this moment. You are in heaven as you love and help your fellow man; and you are in hell as you seethe in anger, jealousy, retribution or the other "sins." It is here and now. "I am that I am."

Once you see beyond your ego and are on The Path, you will be moving toward finding your true self, your true reality, your life's purpose, and your place of peace and happiness.

Redemption is always present and available to you. In the moment that the reality hits you to your core that you have done wrong, and that you can and must make it right; at that moment, you have received redemption. Even if you later lose your way again and again (which we all do), the revelation that you are One with all of humanity and that you hurt yourself and all mankind when you hurt others, will remind you of The One, and cause you to want to return to it. When you actively walk again in The Path of goodness and mercy through your deeds, that is your redemption.

Instead of scolding yourself for having the negative emotion, accept it. It is just your ego, your imperfect ego formed in part by a primitive part of your brain trying to survive. Your ego is busy, active, and often noisy. It is into itself. It will always be there, but you can see it for what it is; thereby neutralizing it and freeing yourself from its control.

It is always talking to you in words such as: "You should not have done that." "You should have said it differently." "He thinks he is better than you." "Go faster." "Be smarter." "Watch out!"

Quiet that voice. There are proven techniques for doing so. You can hear it but not be controlled by it, and eventually, you will be able to ignore it and sense your inner spirit. Your spirit can take you to existence beyond mundane things. That's because life is always changing. Fears and other emotions are always evolving as we go through life. By looking directly and objectively at them, you will better understand where they come from.

Once you are no longer at the mercy of your ego, you will be able to see what you did right and what you did wrong. You will be able to consider how you could have acted or felt differently, so as to create a positive outcome.

You will be able to weigh the pros and cons of succumbing to a negative emotion. Will satisfying that fear, anger, or jealousy keep you happy in the long run, or will it give you a momentary satisfaction that will cause you long-term unhappiness? Those negative emotions really do affect your life negatively. It is worth the time and effort to overcome them. You should act for long-term happiness and for goodness, not for momentary emotional satisfaction.

Maybe you will realize that you have grown far beyond those

events in your life which created those negative emotions, and you needn't fear that fear anymore, or keep that anger that long ago lost its purpose. You need not maintain the jealousy left over from adolescence that can now be put behind you.

The point is that you can control those emotions; they do not have to control you. You can study them with your spirit and your brain and put them into their proper place. Your godly spirit can overcome any aspect of your life that could inhibit you from reaching your full potential. Don't worry about making a stumble or a misstep so long as you are walking in the right direction.

You will gain the power to rise above your egotistical drives. You have the power within yourself to become a purposeful, dedicated, satisfied, godly being. You have the power within yourself to rise above your lesser urges, your vanities, your fears, your faults, your hurts, and your urges for revenge. Those urges are things you have to neutralize in order to grow. That is the purpose of this school called life. To allow us to graduate into wise and spiritual beings.

When you achieve clarity, you will realize that your life has really been a life of love, with mistakes and wrong turns. You mean well, but have been misguided by your embedded hurts. You already have all the goodness you need. What you have to do is remove the obstacles to it.

You will learn to live every moment to the fullest. You will learn to see the best in everything, and every being. You will learn to appreciate the here and now. That will make your unfulfilled desires melt away.

You will learn that this moment is constantly changing. Your life is constantly evolving. You will learn that the reason that you have not been at peace is because you have wanted some parts of your life to go away, and others to stay. You need not hold onto desires. Everything changes. Your feelings are constantly evolving into something different than they just were. It is life. You can't stop it, nor should you try.

Try this exercise. Hold your hand in front of you with your palm upward. Now make a tight fist and hold it for five seconds. Then open your fist and let your hand spread open. Do you feel the tension being released? That is how you will feel when releasing your tense negative emotions and facing life with openness and generosity.

It is within your power to either continue a negative cycle or through love start a positive cycle. Don't be sucked into a negative emotion. See through it. Spare yourself the effects that negativity will have upon you. Don't be controlled by evil. Control it. See beyond it. Look down upon it from a higher dimension of understanding.

Recognize when you are about to be sucked into a cycle of evil. See it for what it is. Breathe in the suffering of that other person, and breathe out loving compassion. Send goodness and love into the world. Take a negative cycle and turn it into a positive one.

You will be happy and wise. People will love and respect you. What is it the Beatles said? "The love you give is equal to the love you get."

Breaking Through to a New Reality

There are different things that can awaken your spirit, and put you on the path to Oneness. When you experience a great loss, despair, depression, or tragedy, you can lose faith in the assumptions and beliefs upon which you have always relied. You can become disillusioned with life. That disillusionment can jolt you out of your complacent normal way of thinking and acceptance of the world-as-it-is, and allow you to consider a new life path that you would have otherwise never considered. It can also allow a revelation to occur within you. It is the "darkness before the dawn" truism that accounts for a large proportion of how revelations, or self-awakening experiences, occur within people.

In 1969, Elizabeth Kubler-Ross wrote a book entitled, *On Death and Dying,* about the stages of loss. Those stages are denial, anger, depression, bargaining, and finally acceptance.

Denial is when one is trying to stick with one's old reality, even after it has gone. That old reality which no longer exists could have been a happy marriage before the spouse died or left, good health which was taken away by some injury or illness, or the diagnosis of a terminal illness. For a while, that person tries to continue to live with the only reality that person has known, within which that person feels security, and in which he or she has become comfortable. That person tries to retain the old security, comfort, or happiness. He or she grasps desperately to that old reality even though it has gone.

Then, at last, realizing the loss, that person may get angry at life and try to find someone to blame for that loss. Then they may begin to bargain with life, fantasizing that becoming a better person will bring back the old accepted reality. But at some point they realize that security, comfort, or happiness is only in his or her memory, and no longer exists. That person accepts that his or her old comfortable reality is gone. Life is now empty. That person's hopes and dreams are gone. He or she is adrift, having been disconnected from the old anchor; his or her old hopes, beliefs, and assumptions.

That recognition throws that person into depression, desperation, and despair; into an unacceptable level of unhappiness. That person becomes disillusioned with life and his or her reality, and discards it. It is that disillusionment and desperation which allows that person to accept the new reality which he or she would never have considered in that person's old life. It is a new beginning.

That is the process through which many people receive an epiphany; a revelation, a change of life. They must be set adrift from unquestioned belief in their old realities before they will accept consciousness-raising new ones. That process continues to be a very common way through which people find their inner spirit. It is the revelation referred to in descriptions of religious experiences. It is the breaking through of a reality barrier into a higher consciousness.

Revelation does not have to come as a result of trauma. It can also occur when you have to muster great courage or when you are inspired by an idea, an action, a cause, or an event (like my experience at the 1969 March on Washington). Being inspired to be in service to a cause greater than yourself enlarges you, and reduces the chances that your ego will interfere with your pursuit of a life of great value.

Another way to break through into higher and higher states of consciousness is through meditation, which was probably the kind of "prayer" which allowed Buddha, Jesus, Muhammed, and others to achieve their higher consciousness. The regular practice of meditation eventually allows you to look through and beyond your normally accepted reality. It is your accepted reality which has controlled you with its reactive emotions and beliefs. Through regular meditation you can learn to objectively observe those reactive emotions and beliefs and see them for what they really are, thus removing their power over you.

Through the insight and clarity brought by that inner calm and openness, you will be able to look objectively at those inappropriate emotional reactions of yours which have brought you such unhappiness and have been a hindrance to you achieving your life's goals. Additionally, through that insight and alertness, you will begin to recognize the real you, not the artificial part of you which has sought fame and fortune and has brought you feelings of jealousy, hatred, and insecurity, but the higher and deeper part of you through which you will find happiness and your life's true meaning.

You can purposefully and regularly meditate in order to still yourself and connect with your inner spirit. Shutting out the noise and vibration of Earthly existence allows you to become in touch with your inner spirit and makes you receptive to receiving precious and astounding insights and revelations. The more you practice being receptive, the more likely you will receive revelations.

I meditate more frequently and for longer periods of time, when I am on a beach vacation with nothing much to do. I can spend most of each day on the beach uninterrupted by life's duties, reading spiritual books and drifting into a state of meditation to one extent or another. My inspirations come more frequently and with more profundity during such times of extended meditation.

Revelations cause your consciousness to leap to a higher under-standing, like walking out of a cave into the sunlight. Great revela-tions happen suddenly and bring you through a threshold into another state of being. Think of Moses at the burning bush, Mohammed in the cave, or Paul on the road to Damascus. It can happen to you, too. Some can be seminal, like mine in 1969 when I understood what it was to be One, and why we should do unto others that which we want them to do unto us. I will later in this book discuss meditation and the techniques for getting you to that inner-most place, and putting yourself in a position where revelations are more likely to occur.

Regular meditation encourages enlightenment, because you will grow to see life more clearly. You will become more receptive to the lessons to be learned from experiences and ideas. You will actively seek out new concepts and experiences.

Change happens. You can't avoid it. Don't fear it. Life is always unfolding. Help your life to unfold in a positive direction.

HOW WILL YOU KNOW WHEN YOU HAVE FOUND SPIRITUAL ENLIGHTENMENT?

St. John of the Cross said: "He who truly arrives there cuts free from himself; all that he knew before now seems worthless, and his knowledge so soars that he is left in unknowing transcending all knowledge." [1]

You will be certain. You will just know that you are within the universal spirit some call God. It is like nothing on earth. It is a simple yet complete knowingness. And you will know it with absolute certainty, with a certainty that it is more real than the "reality" of the world in which you have lived your entire life. You will actually know with ultimate certainty that it is the only complete reality.

You will see that you are a true spirit and that there are no illusions. There is no effort, no form, no distinction, no attachment, no fear, and no desire. You will be in absolute peace and absolute love. You will have absolute understanding. You will have transformed from the wave into the water.

You will know that it has always been within you, but that you just had not known how to sense, or "see" it. Your soul's eye had not yet opened. You will realize that your "seeing" is with your awareness, not your eyes. You will understand that people who deny the existence of an all-knowing and all-encompassing spiritual dimension that transcends the physical have merely not yet learned to perceive the spiritual life force within themselves.

You will know that you are not here by chance. You will know that there is a profound meaning and purpose to life. It is something bigger than just you. You will know that it is so profound that it could not be just by chance. You will know that your life is so much more than the progression of your body. You will know that your life is not limited by your body.

You will realize that the universe is a living presence, which is infinitely good, and that one's spirit continues beyond human death. It must! It is far too monumental to be snuffed out when your mere physical body, it's earthly vehicle, dies.

I use the word "good" for lack of a better word, because Ultimate Reality is beyond the concepts of good or bad in the Earthly life. It is at the essence of both good and bad. It is the universality that allows you to gain spiritual progress from both the "good" and "bad" events of your life. Within Ultimate Reality is the understanding that it is always evolving. Life is always evolving. It is like walking on a path. Even though the path is always changing, you know it is The Path.

In Buddhism, it is said, "God is not the destination; it is the path." You must perpetually live on the path of loving-kindness and understanding. All of us have it in us to find The Path of Oneness. It is a matter of how to look, which will be explained further in this book.

Does The Path ever end? Does it have a conclusion? No. As you get closer to the destination, your path gets wider and wider until it encompasses all of the universe. It overlaps everyone else's path. It just melts away into Oneness. It becomes so second nature that it fails to be a consideration. It just is!

"I am that I am."

Spiritual enlightenment is not a destination, because if you think you have arrived at God or Nirvana, you will have lost it. You will become arrogant, and proud, rest on your laurels, stop opening yourself up, and stop changing. You will harden yourself, look down upon people who you feel have not reached your level of spirituality, thereby losing your connection with them, and losing your Oneness. Here I have to give Tyrone the credit. When I was effusively exclaiming to him that I had reached the ultimate destination, he merely said to me: "Do not confuse the signposts for the destination."

You will realize that the destination is The Path, and that The

Path is the destination. You are not seeking something just beyond your fingertips and in the future. You are already there. The Path is here and now. It was here all along, but you did not know it. As Jacob said when he awoke from his "dream" of being connected to God, "Surely God was in this place, but I, I did not know." [2] Jacob realized that God, the spirit of unity within him, had always been within him, but he had not been able to recognize it until that moment.

"There is no path to happiness: happiness is the path."–Buddha

It is not something that you achieve by striving for it. It is nurtured, not pursued. How is it nurtured? By regularly ignoring the busy world around you and immersing yourself in your spirit. In Tao, it is called "effortless effort." Open yourself up to the beauty of the moment and it will find you. All you have to do is notice it.

It is Not Separate from Everyday Life

The transcendent existence of which I speak is not separate from your Earthly life. After all, isn't the proposing of an existence that is separate from daily physical life itself the making of a distinction? We are considering an awareness that sees beyond distinctions. After all, it is unity itself: The One. So, let us also let go of that final distinction.

The Absolute Understanding of which I speak is not distinct from physical life but incorporates physical life within it. It permeates physical life. It is like a cube of salt which has been dissolved in water. It cannot be seen, but it is everywhere.

Moses, Jesus, Buddha, Muhammed, and so many others, after becoming enlightened and entering The One, did not stay separate from everyday life. They reentered that life more forcefully than ever in order to spread the knowledge of The One to humanity. So, let it be learned from the lives of so many enlightened people that the physical world is of The One, just as the wave is of the water.

Yes, the wave has characteristics that separate it from other waves, but it cannot be denied that at its essence the wave is water.

And in that way, at your essence, you are a spirit that merges with other spirits to form a sea of spirits – The One.

While I was living with Tyrone in the midst of spiritual wonder, I remember a time when I was parking my car on a side street at the end of the day. Before I left the car, I sat and pondered my future direction. How would I live my life now that I had seen the light?

I saw two paths. Should I give up being a lawyer and become a monk, separate from day-to-day worldly experience and dedicate my life solely to learning more deeply about the unity of life? But I saw the examples of Jesus and Buddha. Once having had the veil lifted from them and seeing the glorious unity of life, they did not become solitary, living out their life in the ecstasy of the pure light. They returned to the world and used what they had experienced to help others to experience The One.

So, I decided I would continue living a worldly life, but in The Way of The One. I eventually became a divorce lawyer. I found people at the lowest point of their life, and I helped them through it to again be able to trust, gain confidence in themselves, and find happiness and love. I dedicated my professional life, not to winning, but to finding an equitable solution with as little discord as possible.

Now, even after having been within The One, there are times when you will become lost from the revelatory experience. That is part of the natural process of life on this Earth. You are human! This, after all, is Earthly life with its obstacles, pressures, and stresses. The necessary pressures and obligations of Earthly existence drag us down from our absolute consciousness. Day-to-day life churns up and muddies the waters of your mind. It obscures the spiritual light within your soul. Even when you have mastered the practice of connecting with the eternal, it is inevitable that you will come back into Earthly existence to earn a living and perform the necessary obligations of life on earth.

However, you will be transformed. You will have seen The Light, The Way, The One. You will live your life differently.

As you meditate regularly over a continued period of time, the state of Pure Being or awareness you regularly enter will become more and more infused within your regular mind until eventually it will become so significant within your worldly thinking that you will become wiser, more empathetic, and kinder toward all you are with.

Even though the necessities of everyday life will cause the transcendent aspect of your Absolute Understanding to fade, lessons you have learned will stay with you. At those times, you may not retain your ecstatic direct clear Absolute Understanding of your profound nature, but you will remember its lessons and its importance with your intellectual memory, and you will understand the principles you have learned.

Although you cannot reach enlightenment through your intellect, once you have realized the infinite, your intellect will be forever changed. Once you attain enlightenment, you will know that it permeates every aspect of your life and will thereafter govern your actions and attitudes.

Even though you regularly meditate, life's tragedies will periodically befall you. That is part of the plan. Those tragedies actually do help you along your spiritual journey. Experiencing ugliness helps you recognize and appreciate beauty, as experiencing mediocrity helps you recognize genius.

Even if life's trials and tribulations bring you down from the ecstasy of your connection to the pure Oneness, you will remember that when you were connected with your pure spirit, it was the most profound experience of your life. That realization should drive you to continue following The Path in your everyday life.

In order to prevent the steady erosion of your spiritual awareness, you must set aside the necessary time each week, but preferably every day, to reconnect with your inner spirit. Keep regularly praying, or meditating. For instance, the kind of praying or meditating that you learn about in this book.

As you continue to open yourself up to your spirit through meditation, you will eventually again get closer and closer to The One, become wiser and wiser, calmer and calmer. You will again be more and more able to objectively observe your attachments, fears, jealousies and desires, therefore being better able to control them. The veil of your ego will again become thinner and thinner, and easier to see through. You will again become more and more loving toward your fellow beings. The longer you regularly connect with your spirit, the more likely you will again receive inspirations and epiphanies, leading you to higher and higher levels of understanding until the revelations eventually catapult you beyond human understanding.

When you find your Oneness again after letting it fade, and you are again within serene ecstasy, it will be like finding it for the first time. It will be fresh and newly relevant to where you are in life — a new revelation. How sweet spring is after we have endured the winter! What a sweet rebirth.

But when you look for the Oneness again after losing it, you cannot find it in the same place as you did earlier in life. You have grown. You have learned the heart of the stage of enlightenment you have attained. To find Oneness anew is to find a new answer to a new place in your life — A higher stage of enlightenment. That is as it should be. It will be a new beginning. A new revelation! It will be an epiphany, an "Aha" moment. The old revelation is already known, and cannot be revealed again in the same way. That is why it is so important to be open to new understandings and not be fixed in your old reality.

New revelations build upon the prior ones. Each time, the Oneness you find in a new revelation will bring you closer to full enlightenment, closer to total wisdom and love, and closer to your life's purpose.

Until now we have discussed what The One is, and have referred to the meditative techniques through which it can be found. I will now teach you those techniques.

TECHNIQUES FOR GETTING TO YOUR INNER SPIRIT

Keep the Sabbath

You have it in you to find the path to Oneness. It is a matter of how to look. How should you look? If you want to live a life inspired by your connection to the Oneness, you must set aside a daily or weekly period to regularly connect with your inner spirit.

"Remember the Sabbath day by keeping it holy. Six days you shall labor and do all your work, but the seventh day is a Sabbath to the LORD your God." — Exodus 20:3

The command to keep the Sabbath was one of the Ten Commandments given to us through Moses. That commandment goes on to say: "Surely you must keep my Sabbath, for it is a sign between me and you throughout your generations that you may know that I am the Lord who sanctifies you." — Exodus 31:13. You must keep the Sabbath so that you may "know the Lord," so that you may find and maintain your connection to The One.

The people who wrote the Bible were inspired by their inner Oneness. Therefore, they knew from experience that in order to maintain their connection with their inner Oneness, they had to regularly quiet themselves from their day-to-day tasks so that they could become receptive to their subtle inner spirit. They knew what they were talking about. It was the Oneness within them, their holy inner spirit, which inspired them to introduce the Sabbath commandment.

What did the enlightened writers of the Bible mean by it? Keeping the Sabbath, or resting from your everyday "labors," means to allow your mind to escape from your Earthly worries and responsibilities. The Sabbath is a moment out of time. Different traditions call it praying, or meditating, and describe various ways to open yourself up to your inner spirit, The One within you. Once you experience the Oneness, regular praying or meditating will maintain your connection to it. It will keep you close to your inner One, help you keep the other Commandments, and live a good and happy life. Without regularly meditating, the feeling and clear sight of The One within you will gradually fade away.

Connecting with your pure spirit brings you above your worldly troubles and any psychological hang-ups you may have. While psychotherapy tries to help you understand the causes of your hang-ups, your spiritual connection will cause them to become insignificant. They become unimportant and cease to control you.

Pure Being and the relative world are lived simultaneously and one is not a barrier to the other. Regular transcendental meditation will bring the eternal Oneness closer to your worldly brain. Such practice will more and more infuse the understanding of Oneness into your worldly thinking. You will become wiser and more balanced in your general approach to life. You will become a nicer, better person who reacts to fewer negative impulses.

Through your soul going back and forth from the world of relativity to the transcendental world, and back again over and over, your understanding of the essential nature of being will deepen, and your mind will gradually become more aware of its essential nature. The more that happens, the more the awareness of being will stay within you when your mind is in the world of relativity, and the more Pure Being will become incorporated into your life on earth.

How to Pray or Meditate

Meditation is a form of prayer. Meditating is a time proven technique which has been developed over thousands of years to help you connect with your Oneness. It helps you shut out the noise and clatter of everyday life and calm yourself down, so that the Oneness within you can be sensed. This must be done regularly in order to prevent it from fading away by being drowned out by the noise, rush, and pressures of everyday life. Doing it regularly will make it progressively easier and easier to transform your consciousness into a meditative state.

Unless you regularly connect with your Oneness, you will eventually lose your spiritual inspiration, and it will become only an intellectual memory of a great experience you have had in the past. It is best to connect with your Oneness every day, and it does not have to be for a long period of time.

Prayer is not a spectator event. It is not sitting in a house of worship reading from a text to which you cannot relate, and watching and listening to others. Prayer is not asking for favors from some omnipotent being. It is not something you recite without lingering to understand its spiritual meaning. Also, praying and other religious rituals cannot be allowed to become merely habitual, an end in themselves; going through the motions. Allowing that to happen will limit you and will prevent you from finding your true infinite nature. Through prayer you feel the presence of God, your Oneness with all things. Not a humanoid God, but the Oneness of all, known by some as God and by others as pure awareness. It is through this connecting with your spiritual core that you find the inspiration and meaning of your life.

It can be done anywhere. The nature of the Oneness is that it is found not in the heavens, or necessarily in a house of worship, but within yourself. If you search outside for God, you will be forever searching. If you seek God within your heart, you will find the umbilical cord that connects you with your eternal Oneness.

Praying or meditating sensitizes yourself to that feeling within yourself that opens up the world of the spirit which has always been within you. It is not of time and space. It is, in fact, the peaceful yet fully aware state in which you find yourself when you free yourself from time and space. Remember that the peace you have been seeking is already within you. It is not a destination, an achievement, or something for which you strive. It is not something which may come in the future. It is present and available to you right here, right now. You just have to learn to feel it within yourself.

Also remember that it can't be found with your thinking mind. It is insight. A pure recognition without thought. A revelation. An awakening.

Just let yourself float with it. Just open yourself to it. You will discover that this is the place where awareness and revelation take place, where you can discover your true nature, and your true purpose. You will feel a calmness, an inner quietness. Through that inner quietness you make yourself receptive to sensing The Oneness within you

It is a gradual process. The One will not come to you at the beginning. You must regularly open yourself up to your spirit by using the techniques described in this book and elsewhere. It will eventually come. Don't seek it. Just make yourself open to it. It will find you. The door will open to you. The door to your divine spirit. To your Path. To your inner awareness.

Neuropsychological researchers in the first portion of the twenty-first century discovered that people with significant injuries to their right parietal lobe expressed a feeling of greater closeness to a higher power. The right parietal lobe's primary function is to understand the spatial relationships between objects one sees. Recognizing patterns is essential to problem-solving, a trait that allowed early humans to survive and advance within the physical world.

However, the right parietal lobe also draws attention to our separateness from others, our place in relationship to others. Damage to the right hemisphere of the parietal lobe results in a loss of imagery and visualization of spatial relationships. Interestingly enough, these researchers also found that impairment to that portion of the brain decreases one's focus on the self. [1]

Using Effortless Effort

The purpose of meditating or praying is to lull the spatial and analytical parts of your brain so that the intuitive portions of your brain can be felt. Material life is tough, active, and urgent. It tends to hide the more subtle presence of your internal eternal self: Turn off the TV so you can hear your heart.

When you begin meditating, you will start in the material world, but through continued meditating you will connect to your inner self, to your Oneness. At the beginning, you will be trying to connect with your Oneness. As you practice and become more successful, you will find yourself no longer trying. After all, trying is an act of the material world. It will keep you in the physical world. That's because trying comes from your ego and the world of the intellectual mind.

Let it go. Don't try. By trying you are seeking something you do not already have. You are assuming that what you want is not already here and now. It is and always has been here and now. You will attain it by allowing openness and harmony to overcome you, by letting yourself be absorbed into it. Just be open and receptive. Let it come to you. It will. Life longs for life. If you open yourself to it, your spirit will find you. It has been waiting for you. You just have to sensitize yourself to it. Just let it emerge.

Enter into loving awareness. You will grow into opening yourself up to perceptions which you did not previously sense. You will morph into an open concentration. You will become open and receptive.

Remember that in Tao it is called "effortless effort." Just open yourself up to the beauty of the moment and it will find you.

Since each of us is an individual, each of our paths to the Oneness begins in our own way, from our own place and from our current level, or stage, of consciousness. It is influenced by our family's religion, ethnic heritage, our own life experiences, and the stage of our soul's development.

Inspired teachers from many traditions have taught us in slightly different words that there are many paths to the top of the mountain, but they all lead to the same place. At the core of religious, spiritual, and even humanistic, agnostic, and atheistic beliefs, is the same thing. It is lovingness, Oneness, feeling the unity of all.

Aren't you greater when you are a part of a cause or purpose larger than yourself? You become inspired to greater goals. When you feel the spirit of the Oneness, you will be drawn to follow it. It will lead you from your surface individuality to the universal spirit deep within you. It will free you of self-centered thoughts, of your ego. You must not focus on the differences between your path and that of others. In order to be at one with The One, you must look beyond the differences to the commonality within all paths. Within all people.

Don't think about it. Explanations will not help you. They satisfy the rational mind, and the rational mind is not the path to Oneness, to higher consciousness, to spiritual enlightenment. As I have said, The One cannot really be understood intellectually, it must be felt, sensed, "revealed." It is intuitive.

The Old Testament says that at the moment when Moses was on the mountain receiving the Ten Commandments, he was within an impenetrable cloud of smoke. [2] He and his fellow Jews could see nothing with their physical senses, but received the Ten Commandments through spiritual awareness. You as well must lull your intellectual mind in order to be inspired by the Oneness. In order to become sensitized to the subtle inner light within yourself, your spiritual nature.

Think of a star in the sky. During the day, when there is much ambient light energy from the sun, you cannot see the star. It is only at night when the sun disappears that the star, which has always been there, is perceived. Your everyday life is loud, and the subtle music of the eternal is very hard to hear above its din. Listen to it, it comes from the Eternal. Eventually, continued regular meditation will allow you to more and more sense the presence of your inner spiritual nature

"The world is won by those who let it go."—Lao Tzu [3]

The spirit may open to you when you least expect it, but it is more likely to happen when you have quieted yourself and have become open and clear. Again, it is not found through intellectual reasoning, but by inner calm and clear openness.

You sense it with your spiritual eyes. What some people have called the opening of the inner eye. Many people have described it as a light, because light is a very good metaphor for it. It is like turning on the light in a dark room and seeing it for the first time. But it is not a light in the Earthly physical sense of the word. It is an illumination of your consciousness. An awakening, a recognition, a realization.

It can also be described as an opening. Your being opens up for the first time in your life. It opens to a reality that is more real than the Earthly reality you have experienced up to then.

Buddha first tried extreme methods such as starving and depriving himself to reach this state. He eventually found his Oneness through not trying. He found it through balance and from quieting the forces of the physical world. You, therefore, will not find your true self through extremism or through hard effort. It is the opposite. You will find yourself when you are at balance. You will not find it when you bounce back and forth between one extreme attempt and another, but when you find peace at the place where your Earthly vibrations are at a minimum.

It may be a new place for you, but it is not a scary place. Quite the contrary. In that place you will find yourself at peace with yourself and happy. You will have no fear of new ideas and will be totally open to people with different ideas and lifestyles. You will have lost your insecurities. You will see the value and beauty in all people and in all things. You will notice that people respect you and will be drawn to you.

Using Music as an Aid

Praying or meditating often involves chanting or singing. That is not by accident. It helps lull your thinking brain—your analytical self—

and helps your spiritual self to come forth. It sets up a vibration within you that lulls your active intellectual brain so that the subtle, spiritual part of yourself can more easily come into the forefront of your awareness.

If you are in a chanting environment, such as in a religious service, and do not know the words to the chants, hum the tune to yourself. The vibration is important to open you up to your inner spirituality. A psychologist I once knew described the process of chanting while praying as a technique for suppressing your brain's analytical parts so as to allow the intuitive parts of your brain to come forth. Then, while in that spiritual state during a religious service, you should explore the spiritual meaning within the books in front of you.

Listening to music does the same thing as chanting or singing. Listening to calming or inspiring music is similar to chanting. Personally, I listen to the "Tenku" album by musician Kitaro. It has no words. Some of the pieces are inspirational, like soaring among the clouds, and others are calming, like listening to the waves by the ocean. The first time I heard it I was in a bookstore. I had opened and was reading the Hindu holy text, The Bhagavad Gita. I found myself not just reading the words of the story, but being drawn to the spiritual meaning behind it. I realized it was the music playing in the background which had drawn me out of that Earthly moment in the bookstore and into the spiritual realm. I asked what was playing and immediately bought it. I try to listen to it in the background whenever I am alone reading a spiritual text.

After having listened for years to my music while meditating, I am able to get into a meditative state faster and easier. It makes it much easier for my consciousness to remember its mindful frame of mind. Just calmly listening to that music while deeply breathing automatically brings me there. It is like when a musician "gets in the groove" and he is so far into the music that he forgets himself. Or when you are so far into your dancing that the steps just come without thought or effort. In that state, it seems you use no effort, and you can't get it wrong. "To worship God is to forget the self." [4]

Smoking marijuana can also be helpful up to a point. For the person who is already intuitive, it greatly enhances your intuitive sense. For others, it can open that sense in you for the first time in your life. If you don't yet know how to connect with your spiritual sense, this can bring it out. It lets you know what it is that you are looking for. Then, once you know what it is and that it is within you, you can more easily find it.

People who have smoked marijuana report that doing something as mundane as biting into an apple becomes a wonder. It is like eating an apple for the first time. You wonder at its freshness, how its tree grew from a little seed. You experience its crispness and lusciousness as if you are a child tasting it for the first time, but with the wisdom you have gained through life. It is so tasty, so juicy. It amazes you after all these years of taking it for granted.

You can see a piece of art and experience it to a depth you had never before imagined. You can see a piece of expressionist art, and understand it for the first time.

You can see previously unseen meaning behind thoughts and ideas. You see new wonder and beauty behind events and things. You see with new insight the ideas which you had previously merely looked at and glossed over without a thought. It can be valuable as an aid to gaining new insight and opening up your spirituality.

It is also dissociative. That means that it takes you out of your habitual way of thinking — your ego. It lets you step out of your own ego and look back at yourself. You are not held captive by your usual preconceived beliefs, memories, and life experiences. Rather, it allows you to realize things in a way you could not have done so while in your customary egoistical state. You would have brushed them off without even considering them and would not notice that you are dismissing a new idea without consideration. It is similar to the previously discussed effect of trauma upon your ability to think beyond preconceived notions, but without the trauma. Using marijuana while reading the Bible or other spiritual texts will allow you to more easily gain the profound spiritual meaning behind the words. You will see profound meaning you otherwise would not have seen.

But it can only take you so far. It can befuddle and block the mind. That is why you should never use marijuana while at work, driving, or using any machinery. It is a tool of meditation. When on marijuana, you can experience a great insight, and then immediately forget it. The more eye-opening the realization, the quicker it leaves your consciousness. That is because it is very hard for the brain to accept such an eye-opening idea. The brain cannot handle it; therefore, it tries to push it away as soon as possible. Therefore, if a revelation comes to you when you are meditating with marijuana, have a paper and pen with you and quickly write it down. Otherwise, you will likely forget it. That is a negative aspect of marijuana. When you are in the midst of receiving the most profound inspiration, it leaves you.

Later, when you are no longer under the influence of marijuana, read those notes you wrote. Some will seem crazy or too difficult to understand. They can be discarded. Others will be a revelation to you, and food for greater contemplation. They could change your life.

Becoming Alert to The Moment:: The Mechanics of Meditation

While praying or meditating, if closing your eyes enhances the feeling, close your eyes. The goal is to allow a direct connection with your spiritual self.

In the beginning, if keeping your eyes open and looking at a beautiful sanctuary or natural scene, such as the stars or the shore of the ocean, enhances your closeness to your spiritual nature and puts you in awe of a presence greater than everyday life, do whatever enhances that state of being. Eventually you will pass beyond that presence and close your eyes in order to not be distracted by the Earthly things in sight. You will forget yourself and feel the Oneness of all. You will transcend this Earthly life and enter the spirit of God, pure awareness, the Infinite.

Meditating upon the awesome vastness of a scene such as the ocean or the sky can draw you toward a feeling of infinity and the appreciation of limitlessness. Eventually you will experience limitlessness within you. Meditate on your limitlessness, the true you. Meditate on how your limitlessness permeates and merges with that of everyone and everything.

This "praying" is the act of experiencing God, of Universal Love, the unity of all. It recharges your batteries so that you can bring Universal Love into the way you live your life.

When meditating, sit comfortably so as to minimize the diversion caused by aches and pains. Use a cushion if that helps. Sit with good posture and erect spine. Be relaxed but alert. You want to be alert to the moment, not what happened in the past and not what you want to happen in the future. Once you become calm, while breathing try focusing on parts of your body. Begin by focusing your attention on the bottom of your feet. Feel the floor beneath them and how the floor touches them. Feel how your knees are bent. Feel how your bottom is touching the seat of the chair. Feel how your back is against the back of the chair. Train your awareness on your hands for a while. Feel the stillness of your hands resting upon your still body. Allow yourself to become immersed in the stillness of your body.

Now focus your attention on your breath. Close your eyes and begin to breathe deeply, slowly, and steadily. While you are breathing, be sure to keep your back straight and your head and neck aligned with your spinal column. Relax all the muscles in your hands, arms, shoulders, back, and legs. Breathe very deeply and slowly so that you can feel your chest expanding and contracting. Such deep breathing makes it more likely that you stay focused on your breathing, rather than your thoughts. Become alert to the moment. Feel your breath entering and leaving. Feel the cool air entering and the warm air leaving. Focus upon the feeling of your breath leaving and entering. Think of the air leaving your body as the exiting of your

Earthly troubles, and of the fresh air entering your body as a calmness entering you.

Four to six seconds in, four to six seconds out. Breathe in for a long four to six counts, then breathe out for a long four to six counts. Breathe in a long breath, being conscious that you are inhaling a deep breath. Do it until your abdomen expands. Then breathe out all the air from your lungs, remaining conscious that you are exhaling. Do it while feeling your abdomen contract. Continue to focus on each breath in and each breath out.

For the beginner, it might be easier to ignore external and internal stimuli if you concentrate your vision on one point on the wall in front of you. Just concentrate your vision, and breathe in and breathe out repeatedly. Slowly and deeply. Alternatively, it may be easier to ignore outside stimuli by sitting in a dark room. Also, meditating in the same place and at the same hour each time helps you more easily and quickly get into your meditative state. Your mental body will remember where it is and what it is to do. Use whatever methods work best for you.

In the beginning, you may prefer to breathe through your mouth because it is easier to keep your attention on your breath while breathing through your mouth – it is easier to feel your breath that way. Once it becomes second nature to you, you can breathe through your nose or mouth, whichever is more calming to you and keeps your attention on your breath. More advanced meditators tend to breathe through their nose. Once it has become ingrained, it will become much easier.

Focusing only on your breathing is important. Long breaths help you keep your concentration on your breath. Also, deep breathing relaxes you and infuses more oxygen into every cell of your body. It enhances both your awareness and your body.

Feel the air as it goes in and as it comes out. Focus on that. Some people count as they breathe in, and again as they breathe out. That can make it easier to keep your concentration on your breaths. If you lose count, no problem. Just start breathing again with the counts.

After counting to the same number over and over as you breathe in and breathe out, it will become automatic and natural. If it makes it easier for you to keep focused on your breath, you can instead substitute a spiritually enhancing phrase or chant; saying it as you breathe in, and repeating it as you breathe out.

Keep focusing on your deep steady breathing, and eventually a calm will come over you. When the water is calm, you can see deeper.

Just be still, and open yourself up. Keep breathing deeply, slowly, and steadily. Free your mind from Earthly hindrances such as anxiety, worry, fear, and anger. Feel your anxiety and tension leave you as you exhale. Don't think. Concentrate on your breath. Breathe in, breathe out, breathe in, breathe out. There is no set timeframe. Breathe until a calm comes over you and you feel lifted and are floating.

As you are in your state of stillness, your mind will try to intercede. It will worry about what has to be done later. It will be angry over what someone did to you that morning. Just recognize it for what it is. It is your mind trying to intercede. The ego is a pesky thing that way. Just go back to focusing on the feel of your breath going in and out, in and out. You will return to the stillness.

As another Earthly distraction creeps in, be aware of it, but don't let it take hold of you. Acknowledge it, and know that it is not you, "Oh, a distraction just crept in." Just accept that it is there and that it can be there without interfering with your focus on your breathing. Do not think about it. You can observe it objectively without becoming a part of it, getting caught up in it, believing it, or without feeding or fighting it. Look beyond that thought and become again aware of just the moment. That thought does not control you. It is there, but it can be observed objectively and without emotion. It is not the real you.

Let the distraction arrive freely and don't get involved with it. Just notice it objectively and continue on with your meditation. If you don't get involved with it, the distraction will float away just as easily as it came. Don't actively try to get rid of it, because it will then suck you in. You will be feeding it. Just let it go and return to calm awareness. Draw your attention back to your breath entering and leaving, entering and leaving. Just keep focusing on your breaths.

Don't be disappointed in yourself that your mind repeatedly wanders. You are making progress. Before you began meditating, when your mind wandered, you didn't even notice it. You were just sucked into its reality. You weren't even conscious of it happening. You are making progress. You are expanding your awareness, your consciousness.

The Buddha once told the following story which illuminated the kind of focus found in effective meditation. Once a famous dancer came to a village and the people were excitedly mingling and waiting expectantly to marvel at her abilities. At the same time, a condemned criminal was ordered to cross the village carrying a bowl filled to the brim with oil. He had to concentrate with all his might to keep the bowl steady, because following him was a constable with a sword ordered to cut off his head if he spilled any oil. Do you think he paid attention to the twirling dancer, or the hordes of people milling about?

That is the nature of the alert focus you will learn to have while in meditation. You will learn to focus upon the very nature of what it is upon which you are meditating. You will not concern yourself with what others do, or with what others think. You will be complete within yourself.

Once you have become accustomed to meditating successfully, here is a progressive serious of exercises that may work for you. Each of these steps will take numerous sessions before you will be ready to move on to the next step.

Meditate by fixing your gaze upon a lit candle, a flower, or some-thing else that represents purity and simplicity to you. Once you have meditated upon the candle or flower for a while, you should move your consciousness to just the flame of the candle, just the color of the flower, or to the essence of the representation you have chosen.

Exclude all other perceptions. Now, close your eyes and imagine that same essence without seeing it with your eyes. See it with a sense beyond physical seeing.

After having done the preceding exercise repeatedly for many meditation sessions, you can try to free yourself from even the awareness of what you are doing. Just be there and be simply aware. Not aware of anything; just simply in a state of awareness. Be aware only of boundless empty space.

After a while start seeing with your consciousness, not your eyes. Be aware of your existence and let it float and expand. Let it become spacious and open. Let it expand more and more into the surrounding universe. Let your consciousness remain in that expansive stillness. You will feel the expansiveness of your heart and your inner being expand beyond your body. Your body will even become irrelevant to the expansiveness you feel. After a few minutes, you will become filled with a deep peaceful joy.

Later, having experienced the formless world, you will be ready to experience the final step of awareness. It is known as Pure Being. It is beyond being in the formless world. It is being simultaneously both in the formless world and in the binary world of forms and distinctions. That is Oneness.

After a while you may feel calm and lighter, almost floating, less tied to the Earth. Let it happen. Go with it.

Don't actively pursue it, just let yourself be open to the moment. Remember that it is called "effortless effort." Don't strive. Just let it happen. Eventually it will. You will begin to see things in a new way.

Let yourself be calm, yet alert, and open to all. Be alert not just to the sound of the truck passing, or the air-conditioner humming, but also alert to the lightness you feel within you after the physical world has been allowed to fade away from your attention. Imagine yourself opening up like a blooming flower, opening to the universe.

Don't worry if that opening does not come to you in the beginning. If you keep the practice regularly, your inner senses will open up and you will expand the sphere of your awareness. You will come to realize that all of life is within every moment. That you are connected with all that there is and everything that can be experienced can be experienced here and now. You will realize that in every moment you are permeated with all that there is, and that there are no boundaries.

In the beginning, be content to seek calm attentiveness, joy, and internal peace. Don't strive for enlightenment. It is not something to seek. It already is, and has always been, within you. Through regular meditation, your worldly veneer, your veil, will slowly dissolve, and your spiritual awareness which has always been at your core, will slowly become visible to you. Just let it happen. As I have said, if you actually try to seek it, it will not appear. Just open yourself to it. You will gradually better understand life and yourself. Eventually you will fully understand life, yourself, and others. Remember that such an understanding is already within you. You just have to let it emerge and develop.

It is in this state that you can become sensitive and receptive to feelings, thoughts, and understandings that you just didn't, or couldn't, notice when controlled and distracted by the world. Practicing this exercise regularly will bring you closer and closer, deeper and deeper, to a reality more real than what goes on in the material world. You will begin to gain better insight into your memories of life events, and the concepts and beliefs you have held. You will re-examine your heart, your life. You will discover your greater purpose. Do it correctly, repeatedly, often, and for long enough periods and eventually you will cross a threshold into another dimension.

Be in the present. Once you have learned through concentration on your breath to leave the world behind and free your concentration from everyday life, you can meditate upon things related to whatever stage of spiritual progress you have not yet attained. If, for instance, you are meditating upon being loving and empathetic, and you find that you quickly and easily connect to its spiritual basis, and incorporate it into your life, that is a sign that your soul has already reached that spiritual level. Continue incorporating it into your day-to-day life. At the same time, try meditating upon something else, such as your negative emotions, you not being limited by your body, or your infinite being.

Do not be discouraged if you cannot seem to make headway by meditating on a particular subject. All that means is that you are not ready for it. Keep on meditating and when you are ready to reach a higher stage of consciousness, it will appear to you. It may be something you had looked at many times before, but either did not notice, or did not seek to pursue. All that means is that you had not yet been ready for it.

When within calm alertness, you can learn the true substance of your knee-jerk emotions. When you learn to look objectively and dispassionately at your reactive negative emotions, you will spend less time resenting indignities inflicted upon you and less time on revenge fantasies against inflictions. Try ceasing to identify with those negative emotions by imagining yourself as only being a witness to your mind experiencing negative emotions and thoughts, and know that it is only your mind doing so, not the true you.

Each time you are in deep meditation, allow your spirit to just expand and float. If you do this regularly while meditating, you may feel your spirit floating beyond your body. You may even be able to sense that your body is down below you and that you are looking down upon it, or that your body is finite and that you have expanded beyond it. You may be able to sometimes imagine yourself as not walking, talking, eating, or breathing, but as witnessing yourself walking, talking, eating, or breathing. This will help free yourself of your identity as a body. You are not limited by your body. Your true self, your spirit, is limitless.

If you seriously want to devote yourself to spiritual enlightenment, you should as soon as possible devote one day a week to connecting with your spirit. Your day of rest from the mundane world. When you wake up on that day, begin your steady breathing while still in bed, continue it while showering and brushing your teeth. Breathe deeply in and out, and if a distraction creeps in just ignore it as usual. This is your day of rest. Whatever you do that day, do it in a meditative state.

Keep your talking to a minimum. You can mouth spiritually oriented phrases that enhance your meditative state of mind. You can even cook your meals that day in mindfulness. Eat them calmly and with reverence for the plants and animals who have sacrificed their lives so that you may eat. And don't forget all those truckers. Then go back to enjoying this day of peace. Walk in a garden or by a river, or the sea. Be sure to spend a good part of the day studying spiritual writings while in a meditative state, as described in this teaching.

By short daily meditation sessions, by trying to remember to meditate while going about your usual day, and by dedicating at least one day a week to mindfulness, you will find that your spirit will be ever present in all you do, and you will be the best person you can be. To be successful, every path must involve dedication. You can't make consistent headway by meditating only once a month or less. I strongly recommend finding thirty minutes a day to tune out the world and meditate. It will become a relaxing and refreshing time that you will look forward to.

Just be. Be fully in the present moment even while traversing your day-to-day life. Learn to accord infinite value to every moment of existence.

Try to meditate for thirty minutes every day. Release yourself from your body. Let yourself float with ease. Getting ready for your regular meditation should be like looking forward to getting together with a special friend, or going to a relaxing vacation spot you love.

I am a doer. When I try to relax, I am often antsy, feeling that there is something I should be doing. Not so when I meditate. When I meditate, I am fully content within my silence and calmness. I am disappointed when it ends.

Although meditation has been proven to be the most effective tool for achieving mindfulness, you can practice mindfulness even when not sitting in meditation. You can even use your breathing technique while at work, walking, standing, sitting at your work desk, washing the dishes, or whatever you are doing.

I recommend doing some research and finding a local or web-based regularly scheduled meditation class or group, especially led by an inspirational, relatively ego-less leader. You can benefit from his or her knowledge and experience. Let yourself lose yourself.

Everything is in the present. Think about it. When you are remembering the past or considering the future, you are always in the present moment. You are always only living in the present moment.

Today, this moment, is truly the beginning of the rest of your life. How you are and what you do in this moment will lead to what you will become. At this moment you are free to change your direction by what you do and of what you become aware. In every moment, the past and the future have no power over you, only the present.

Marcus Aurelius said if you separate yourself from the memories of the past and the hopes for the future and avoid ruminating on the present, you enter a calm serenity and benevolence. Keep your consciousness aware of the present moment. Live happily in the present moment. Whatever arises, just be present for it.

Total involvement has a mindless quality. The ego is quiet and you are that which you are doing. Silence allows you to be here and now. Not within the avalanche of talking and gabbing just for the sake of filling the silence.

Embrace what you have when it is here and now. Appreciate the here and now. Pay attention to your thoughts and feelings. Sense the present without rehashing the past or imagining the future.

Meditation is not an effort to control your mind. It acknowledges your mind, yet expands your consciousness beyond it. You do not meditate to create a particular experience, but to provide a space for any experience. You meditate in order to see things the way they are. Meditation is not escaping from life, but learning to stay open to it. Through meditation you will learn that what makes something special is the nature of your awareness of it, not just what you intellectually think about it.

After meditating for some time, you will begin to contemplate your life from a different perspective. You will study the relationship between your true perception and the harmful urges and emotions you have had. You will look at the anxieties that are interfering with your happy life.

You will learn that your fears and kneejerk urges are a part of your ego. You won't fear them or fight them. You will just accept them as a part of your life. You will try to understand them. Where did each come from? When did each start? What exactly is it, a physical feeling or purely emotional? How does it affect you? This will allow you to free yourself from their control.

As you progress, you can also focus your meditation on spiritual progress. Try repeating to yourself in your mind, "I am infinite." Or meditate on the concept of God, or on the unity of all. You will be beyond looking at a point or repeating words. You will be gradually opening the spiritual sense within you. See if you feel your spirituality opening up. Feel the lightness it brings, and the feeling of openness and acceptance.

It is especially helpful to meditate upon the divine qualities of a spiritually enlightened person of the present or past, such as Buddha, Gandhi, Martin Luther King, or Christ. It should be someone whom you especially appreciate and desire to emulate. Do so until you have merged yourself with the spirit of that enlightened person, so that your spirit understands the nature of his or her Oneness.

Keep meditating in that way so that you gradually begin to feel the spiritual basis of each concept, and gradually feel it more continuously and with more intensity. You are on The Path.

You can meditate upon thoughts that are troubling you; realizing of course that they are only thoughts and only your reaction to things. Become aware of their true nature and how they arose in you. Meditating upon a negative emotion of yours will eventually lead to an understanding of its nature. That understanding will free you of its control.

When in a state of calm awareness, you are more able to objectively see your habitual reactions. You should ask yourself, "Is the way I usually react to a certain event an expression of kindness and empathy? Do I react negatively and hurtfully to a person's annoying actions without remembering that he or she could be me at certain times? How would I want to be treated when I act that way?"

Do pain and pleasure control you? They are the winds that will batter you about. You don't have to let them control you. You have learned that they are mere momentary impressions. Consider them deeply. Meditate upon them.

Look at their sources within you. Where did each start? How did it get magnified? Is that a pain which has long since become unimportant? Look at it in the eye clearly. You don't need it anymore. To hell with nostalgia. There is no real reason to worship the past. You owe it nothing. It has held you down for no good reason. You have the power to cast it into the rubbish heap.

Think of the person who has harmed you the most. Think of his or her attributes which you despise the most. Contemplate what makes that person happy and what causes that person to be unhappy. Put yourself into his or her shoes and try to see how that person sees that happiness and unhappiness. Try to imagine that person's hopes and dreams, and from their own viewpoint what causes them to become unhappy and hurtful. Have they been unable to prevent those causes from controlling their life? Consider how that has been also true of yourself. Continue until you feel compassion for that person, and your resentment of that person melts away. Meditate on how you feel compassion for those who are suffering.

Meditate upon your greatest achievements. Why did you do them? Was it entirely to improve the world, or was there some ego involved? Was it done to seek recognition or praise? See how those egoistic impulses lessened the good you were trying to achieve. Contemplate how the aura emanating from egotism can be sensed by others, and thus lower their opinion of you.

Meditate upon the memory and lingering emotions related to a loved one who has died. Contemplate that although they were only temporarily on this Earth, they left an eternal trail of love and goodness which continues on in those who remain.

Meditate upon a thing that you fear losing. It could be health, a person, or anything else you do not want to lose. Now connect that thought to your heart. Feel your love for that person or thing and the pain you would feel if you lost it. Then, with all of your heart, feel compassion for yourself and wish yourself to be free of that pain and grief. Appreciate the happiness you received from that precious thing while it was in your life. Feel compassion for all those who have lost and are within grief. Really feel your appreciation for being in the stream of life — for the things that have given you happiness which have flowed into it and flowed out of it. Remember that the same flow that allowed them to come into your life also allowed them to flow out of it. It is truly the stream of life. You must take the bad with the good and make the most of every present moment. Appreciate every moment. Appreciate what you have.

Light your own torch, which will show you your holy direction in life. Meditate on your daily work. Meditate on how it contributes to the betterment of the world. How it is a cog in the holy wheel of eternal life. It makes no difference what it is so long as it helps and does not hurt. Even cleaning someone's house or picking in the fields is an indispensable contribution to the happiness and well-being of others.

Let your spirit open toward goodness and love. If you can get to that spiritual state for at least thirty minutes every day — maybe in the early morning, on your lunch break, or in the evening, and also for an extended time at least once per week — you are on your way. Eventually you will begin receiving minor epiphanies, and every so often greater ones. You will be moving along the path toward higher consciousness and will be putting yourself in the position to eventually receive that great revelation which will open you into spiritual enlightenment, the ultimate reality.

It does not have to be a very long path to awareness. You can enter the path right now by spending time forgetting the past and being unconcerned about the future. Just be here and now, and breathe deeply. Let your spirit open up to you. Flow with it to that place deep within you.

Not only are you not your body, you are also not your thinking mind. In a state of meditation, you can separate yourself from your thoughts. So, instead of you believing that you are what you are thinking, you can detach yourself from your thoughts and look at them objectively. Not subjectively, as in being within them and believing that everything includes an "I" or "me." But rather apart, looking at them with objectivity and awareness.

You will understand the original misunderstanding or overreaction to an event which initiated the reactive thought or emotion, and thus release its painful hold on you. With such objective awareness of your thoughts, you are more able to see their true sources, and understand why you think and feel the way you do. Once the source of your painful thoughts is understood, you can more easily free yourself from their control. You can see your thoughts without identifying with them as part of your self-concept. You will have entered a state of being that is deeper than thought. You will instead no longer be dragged around by your thoughts. You will merely observe your thoughts with calm awareness.

Continue to let yourself open to deeper awareness. While meditating, say to yourself over and over, "I am aware." But don't just say it, feel it. Let yourself be drawn into it. Let it bring a lightness and happiness to you. Feel your beingness expand beyond your mind, beyond even your body. Let your consciousness float free. Be aware of yourself meditating while in a body and be aware of the world around you.

Your goal is to step out of your ego by not only being aware, but being aware that you are being aware. To lose oneself is to enter absolute beingness and to find eternity. Let your consciousness expand beyond the Earthly plane and into a state of pure and absolute awareness. The truths you receive from the unformed, eternal Oneness within you will automatically contain purity and compassion for all things. The actions you will be caused to perform, and the words you speak from those new truths, will emanate from a beautiful and sacred place and will contain no ego with its damaging urges. They will rather contain within them the power to transcend your doubts and fears, allowing you to move beyond them. You will have the power to accomplish good deeds and bestow harmony and beautiful blessings upon the world.

In this teaching, I cover meditation as a proven effective technique for opening yourself up to your inner spirit. I believe I describe it sufficiently to enable you to use it successfully. I could not, and do not, intend my coverage to be an exhaustive or expert dissertation on the subject. There are many books, videos, websites and teachers through which you can further pursue the subject. Once you have found a teacher, a guru, a guide to which you can relate, use him or her as you would a map to travel to your spiritual destiny.

You will not be able to fully connect with your spirit and discover your life's purpose unless you can see your own personality, wealth, and position objectively for what they are, and become free of their egoistic control over you. It was said in ancient literature that the Devil had great powers and tried to become as great as God. However, the Devil failed at the final step. He was not able to release himself from his quest for control and power: his ego. In spite of his great powers, or because of the way he used them, his greed, lust, and ambition prevented him from being as God.

The "Devil" is a symbol of those "sins" which prevent you from finding your Oneness, and connecting with what some call God. Through regular meditation, and the power of the love within you, you will gradually learn to release yourself from the control of your ego. You will get closer and closer to seeing your true, pure, spiritual self. Love is the means and is the end.

Practicing Oneness in Your Day-to-Day Life

While on the spiritual path toward Oneness, you can reinforce and enhance that journey by bringing it into your normal life. You can devote part of your week to selfless service. You can volunteer at a soup kitchen, visit lonely elderly people at a nursing home, help the injured, teach the illiterate, or choose some other service to which you feel a special connection. By doing this you will be practicing what you are learning. You will be giving and receiving love, the path to God, and to finding your true self. You will receive far more than you give. There is no end to the different ways that you can serve selflessly toward a goal larger than yourself. While serving, you will feel closer to The One, your infinite spirit.

As your spiritual awareness continues to blossom, you may find that opportunities for greater awareness present themselves to you. This is because you will become receptive to situations you probably would have otherwise ignored. There is enough going on in this world so that when you are ready to receive a lesson from the world, it will appear to you. In other words, you will discover the learning events meant for you when you are really ready for them.

You can contribute to your progress by connecting with a spiritually advanced person from whom you can learn. Pursue it. It can be very helpful to let such a person guide you. Such a person is likely to appear when you are ready for it, just as Tyrone appeared to me at just the right moment.

It makes sense that there are self-delusions that are very difficult for you to see by yourself. This is just as the eye is unable to see itself. It may take an enlightened mentor to recognize and help you see those parts of your ego that are the hardest for you to accept.

It is important to put into practice the spiritual wisdom that you have already attained. Put it to work in the world. Become one with it, and experience it in all ways. What is the value of attaining spiritual wisdom if you do not practice it in your day-to-day life? Through that practice, you will merge your life more deeply with the epiphanies you have received. That will make it more likely that you will become available to your next epiphany.

You will most likely make mistakes when applying your newly learned wisdom in the world, and that is good. From those mistakes you will further refine your understanding and gain further wisdom.

Once you find your hidden calling, that goodness unique to you, don't let the minutia of other things get in the way of your fulfilling it. Focus upon it. Enrich your understanding of it through inquiring of those who have lived it, reading books they have written about their experiences, and meditating upon it. Make it your primary focus in life. Do not falter or be diverted by pleasure or pain. Do your best.

Do it for the higher purpose, the higher good. Having done so, you will leave this life with grace and happiness. Do not let the seeking of wealth, praise, or adoration for doing it be your primary motive. That will pollute it and lessen it. That will not allow you to truly fulfill your calling.

Don't fall short. Don't fail. If you find what it is that you can contribute to the world, go after it. Live it. Focus on your purpose and your mind will be tranquil.

Not everyone finds his or her destiny. Life is short and once you find your destiny, you must fulfill it. Feel fortunate. Don't waste it! Make the most of every moment. Make the most of your life.

How to Study Prayers and Religious Texts with Your New Understanding

The Oneness that connects all beings is beyond words. But words can be a springboard to it, catapulting you to that spiritual dimension. Now when you hear or read a prayer, try to think of God as you have learned in this teaching, not as an external being, but as The One, your pure awareness: the spiritual source within all people that unifies them with all.

Wouldn't it be nice to read a prayer that is personally inspiring? Try reading those old religious passages that once had no meaning for you. Read them with the new understanding you have gained. You will see that they were never meant to be taken literally. Read them over and over, and study them until you discover the spiritual meaning within them. You can find your deeper understanding of your inner Oneness within the prayers of all faiths.

You can be selective with the passages you ponder. For example, some parts of the Bible were meant to be a recitation of the rules and regulations of everyday life. Remember that when the Old Testament was compiled and the oral traditions were written, people were living in a theocracy. The priests governed all aspects of life. So, some parts of the Bible were meant to command a relatively uncivilized and uneducated person to follow the rules for staying healthy and peacefully living with others. Yet they can still be very instructive to us, and you can meditate upon their underlying spiritual basis. But they were not meant to be prayers. Other parts of the Bible recite genealogy. They are interesting and helpful to historians, but they were also not meant to be prayers.

Aside from those types of passages, there are many rich passages which can lead you to your spiritual self. Start with those with which you have felt a connection, or which you have felt had a deeper meaning which you could not quite get, or which have been mystifying to you. Don't just read them and continue on. The full meaning will not come all at once. With some passages your understanding will grow deeper and deeper as you recite them over and over and meditate upon them. Discuss them with others. Study them until you see their spiritual underpinnings and the word of God shining through. The wisdom within spiritual texts can help you look deep within yourself, and can guide you toward your godly inner place and your life's meaning and purpose. Much of what I am communicating here came to me while immersing myself in Biblical and other spiritual writings of people who have found The Path.

When I was young, I was taught to understand the Bible literally. That caused me to accept that God long ago had stopped communicating with humans. Those miraculous things happened in the days of the Bible, but they do not happen today. I now know that the spirit of Oneness, known by some as God, still speaks to us through these religious texts, and through life. The people who wrote those words were writing from the spiritual inspiration gained from having connected with their inner godly core of Oneness. In a manner of speaking, God was speaking through them. So, you can study, feel, and meditate on their words in order to find your own spiritual connection, your godly direction, and get closer to The One within you.

It is often difficult to understand the meaning of those words, because they were written hundreds or thousands of years ago, and were written within the context of their times. You must see beyond the idiosyncrasies of their times and places. You may be saying to yourself as you read this that you have tried, and that those old passages are boring, or too difficult. You should study them while in meditation. You may find that you have become miraculously open to them, and can actually connect with their previously hidden insights.

When in the readings you read of the "voice" of God, think of it as the inner inspiration received by the people in the event while they were connected to their Oneness. It is a "voice" from within, not a dictate from an external source, nor an audible roar from a cloud. When you read of acts of God, think of them as acts and perceptions of inspired people while they were connected to their inner Oneness. Heaven is within you after all. Those words were never meant to be taken literally. Words are of this Earth, not of heaven. Words are limited, and the inspired people who wrote them knew that.

Those tales can be interesting, but aside from those that are meant to be just a genealogical or historical recitation, a literal interpretation misses the true value of the story. Take them as teachings of a greater point, such as the parables of Jesus. They are meant to be springboards, catapulting you beyond the words, beyond the physical. Find the spiritual meaning within them. You can find the essence of Oneness in the writings of all religions and of non-religious enlightened people.

Reading the writings of spiritual masters is an entry form to meditation. During the first stage, you read the passage repeatedly so as to find its spiritual truths. Then you meditate upon those truths constantly. Eventually you will no longer ponder those truths, but will spontaneously and intuitively know them.

Remember the traditional Buddhist saying: "Words can be like fingers pointing to the moon. If you continue to look at the fingers, you will never see the moon." Interpret the prayers and the passages in the holy texts with your new understanding, and let that new understanding catapult you to divine inspiration. You must focus on every word and phrase, hovering over it, repeating it, meditating upon it; until you can hear the word of God within it. Until it touches your soul.

For instance, in Psalm 27, David says that "when the wicked, my enemies come upon me and those evil doers feed upon my flesh, they have stumbled, fallen." Do we take this literally? Does this describe some magic power of an almighty super person or force?

Search for the meaning within the words. If someone is so angry as to figuratively "eat the flesh" of another, can you imagine the degree of anger seething within them? Who does that really hurt?

A person who practices loving kindness and "walks in the truth," as David says in Psalm 26, does not walk in fear of evil doers. He that "offers sacrifices of joy" spreads happiness to others. He is within the light of the unity of all. That person will rise above the tumult and the negativity and will be calm, happy, and content, because he understands the nature of hate. He understands that the barbs thrown by the haters cannot really harm him. They in fact really hurt those who do the hating. In order to hate and do evil, a person must really be hurting deeply inside. Thus, they stumble and fall, as in the passage.

Psalm 27 connects with our feelings of doubt and trouble, and shows us how connecting with our loving spirit helps us rise above the negativity and remain happy and content. So, as you study a spiritual passage, let the voice raise from the page and enter your soul. It will provide insight into the nature of something meaningful to you.

Try this exercise:

1. Read a passage literally. Imagine you are involved in what is being described and consider how that would affect your life.
2. Meditate for five minutes.
3. Read it again and consider its hidden spiritual meaning. What is the message?
4. Spend five minutes writing about that spiritual meaning.
5. Meditate upon what you wrote and expand upon your writing.
6. Read the passage again. How does it help your spiritual development?

There are so many books written by people inspired by their revelation of The One. The more you read, especially while in a meditative state, the more you will progress along your path to spiritual enlightenment.

Yes, the spiritual texts can lead you, but it is only you who can make the leap out of your ego to the Oneness. You can be lifted beyond yourself, beyond your ego, closer to the light, closer to enlightenment, away from your petty fears, your jealousies and the things that make you small and unhappy. Your soul includes your personality, but your spirit is the pure Oneness freed from your ego, from desire, and from failure.

You may find that you experience God in a way that you never have before. You may find that you see God for the first time. Not through your physical eyes, but in the way spoken of in the holy books of all spiritual traditions.

Be receptive toward all things. See the beauty in all. Understand that all things of this Earth are impermanent and fluid. Accept the beauty and impermanence of everything. Some of the most impermanent things are the most beautiful, and their impermanence does not lessen their beauty, such as the blossom of a flower or a sunset. Or us. Yes, us. Feel the beauty of all things and have compassion toward them. See the richness and abundance of what you have, what you are, and of all around you. Pursue the meaning in all of life's experiences.

See the perfection, the ultimate beauty, in every moment. Remember that everything that happens is beautiful, even things that are seemingly hurtful or disappointing to you. You will learn from them, and grow wiser. See the best in everything.

All of this should help you get beyond your individual self. You will receive the greatest fulfillment in all you do if you act for the common good, not for self-interest. You will find that you do everything better when acting for a goal greater than yourself. You will be "in the zone."

THE PLACE OF THE TRUE SPIRIT IN YOUR LIFE: FINDING AND LIVING YOUR LIFE'S PURPOSE

Accept all that comes into your life, including the misfortunes such as sickness and death. They, as you know, are usually unavoidable. Learn from them. That is why they are a part of life. Appreciate what you learn from them.

Hesitate and appreciate the little things in life. The crust on bread, the richness of ripe fruit, the joy of a child, the rustling of grass or leaves in the wind, and the calmness of a beautiful landscape.

Turn obstacles into fuel for improvement. An obstacle can either overwhelm you, or you can use it as a learning experience. Learn from that experience. It all depends on how you look at it, your perception of it. Do you see it as being huge and unconquerable, or do you see it as a challenge from which you can learn?

Don't deny, avoid, or hide your grief. It is important that you go through it. After immeasurable despair, you will learn from it. Allow your painful experience to open yourself to a greater awareness.

Those things that bother and worry you really have no hold upon you. They will change before your very eyes. They will soon not be the same as they are now, but will alter and eventually cease to exist. The things that trouble you about them are only a product of your perception and attitude. They are delusions you allow yourself. See beyond those delusions.

When you are within the darkness of loss and despair, pray as I have taught here so that your inner all-knowing spirit will illuminate your tormented soul. It will show you how your loss can be filled, and your despair can be cured. Not by you receiving something, but by you truly realizing that you already have what you feel is missing. It will show you how to perceive all that you already have and how to realize its full importance.

If you choose to not be hurt, then you will not be hurt. Likewise if you do not feel hurt, you have not been hurt. Think about it! It is up to you! At some point, even after experiencing extreme grief, you can become empowered. Long-term you can rise above the twists and turns of banal existence. It is the world as it is. You can accept it and deal with it. You can be happy and successful in the midst of adversity.

Do not sacrifice the long term and deep for the short term and superficial. Keep your holy character as you deal with the world. Don't let evil suck you in.

No matter how long you have been practicing mindfulness or where you are on your path to enlightenment, you will experience happiness and sadness, gain and loss. How it affects you will depend upon what you see in it, your perception of it.

A positive aspect of being within the depths of despair is the knowledge that the only direction from there can only be up. If your life has been in darkness, it is within your power now — at this moment — to light your candle. It is never too late to start your journey.

A person who has attained spiritual enlightenment can see both pain and gain within each other. Pain is a part of gain, because the inevitable loss of gain causes pain. So, every gain includes loss, and every loss includes gain. They are inseparable. Maintain a happy contentment by keeping the long term in your thoughts. Know that gain and loss are both temporary. They both flow through you.

Can you take control of the flow of pain and gain through you? Yes, you will feel the pain and can learn and grow from it. If you realize that both pain and gain, and happiness and sadness, are temporary, you will learn to mitigate both. Don't reject or push away the pain. Just let it naturally change into something positive as you begin to fully understand its true nature. For example, if you receive a windfall of something, you can encourage the flow by being generous and sharing it with others. If you are within loss and sadness, what effect do you think it would have on you to actively console others who are in pain and sadness?

An injury you receive through being careless will in the future remind you to be careful. Did you lose a loved one during the time of COVID? What did that loss and its grief do to you? It probably deepened your resolve to practice the techniques which would keep you safe. These are examples of trimming the sails to weather the storm.

Gain will usually come with stresses and responsibilities, while loss can come with relief from great responsibility. Which is the gain and which is the loss? It comes down to your perception of it, doesn't it? If you can see the gain in the pain and the pain in the gain, you can lead a calmer and more aware life. A life less burdened by your egoistic emotional ups and downs.

There is a wisdom to accepting a bad diagnosis. You will feel the deep grief, but then you can later say, "Life has yet again changed. I will use this as a learning experience and that which I learn from this very bad experience should be quite profound." Open yourself to change. Don't waste a crisis. Conquering a crisis can lead to your most important breakthroughs.

Just because it is fate, does not mean it was decided long ago or has been set in stone. The trajectory of fate is forever bending by events and actions, man-made or not. Fate is forever changing. Your job is to be ready for it. Be ready to trim those sails to make positive use of the wind, no matter what speed or direction it takes.

Despite its ups and downs, the universe has a way of righting itself and slowly but surely moving in the direction of Oneness. You may not realize that at the time of the tragedy, but have faith. "No doubt the universe is unfolding as it should" [1] and you have the power in each moment to shape your own destiny, to turn your life in a loving, productive direction. Perhaps the knowledge and insight you gain from this book will give you the inspiration to do so.

Remember that the world is constantly putting before you the signs and events from which you can use to find your path to enlightenment. Try to recognize them, keeping an open inquisitive mind.

When you are overcome with the fear of losing something, you are already within that fear, therefore you have already lost. So, give up the fear. It is created within you by your ego. Everything is born from change, and that which existed before is the seed of new growth.

Accept all things with appreciation. They have been put in your life to help you along your path to eternal awareness. All things, even suffering and death. The highs and lows of life will always come. It is your faith, flexibility, and patience that will get you through. Have faith that life will always be changing, and what is important is how you deal with life's ups and downs . The benefit of patience is that it allows you to look at your discomfort and gives you the time to meditate upon it so you can get to a place of peace in that moment.

Reinhold Niebuhr wisely wrote: "God grant me the Serenity to accept the things I cannot change, Courage to change the things I can, And the Wisdom to know the difference. Living one day at a time, Enjoying one moment at a time. Accepting hardship as a pathway to peace."

Accept the new things that come into your life and let them transform you. Study them inside and out, and include them in your journey toward the unity of all. Don't be afraid of change. Remember that everything in this world is always transforming at all times. And also remember that something is always born from something that dies. "Life and death are one, even as the river and the sea are one." [2]

Death of our body just follows the flow of nature. The fact that physical things dissolve and then combine and dissolve and combine endlessly is a law of nature. In time it will be your turn to give up your body. It will be converted by nature into food for plants, which will in turn become food for animals, which in turn will become food for your loved ones, again and again. Life is always changing, always unfurling, and evolving.

The ultimate reality treats birth and death in the same way. They are both expressions of life. Although opposite, they evoke similarly profound, extreme emotions. Accepting each as a part of the inevitable flow of life will give you a more balanced and deeper understanding of them both.

Once you are ready for death, you are ready for life. Once you realize that you are universal and limitless, and that your life is not limited by the mere death of your physical body, you will be ready for death, and therefore ready for life. You will do everything as if it were the last thing you are doing in life.

Live as if there is no tomorrow. So true that saying is! Don't leave making things right for some other day. If something is important for you to do, do it now. Schedule your acts by what is most important. Be good today, not tomorrow.

> *Birth is a beginning*
> *And death a destination.*
> *And life is a journey:*
> *From childhood to maturity*
> *And youth to age;*
> *From innocence to awareness*
> *And ignorance to knowing;*
> *From foolishness to discretion*
> *And then, perhaps, to wisdom:*
> *From weakness to strength*
> *Or strength to weakness –*
> *And, often, back again;*
> *From health to sickness*
> *And back, we pray, to health again;*
> *From offense to forgiveness,*
> *From loneliness to love.*
> *From joy to gratitude,*

From pain to compassion,
And grief to understanding –
From fear to faith;
From defeat to defeat to defeat –
Until, looking backward or ahead,
We see that victory lies
Not at some high place along the way,
But in having made the journey, stage by stage,
A sacred pilgrimage.
Birth is a beginning
And death a destination.
And life is a journey,
A sacred pilgrimage –
To life everlasting.[3]

Zen teaches that once you have found Absolute Consciousness, you will return to the Earthly world enthusiastically and with humility. Jesus, Moses, Mohammed, and Buddha did not become solitary monks, spending the rest of their lives basking in their spiritual knowledge. Their spiritual knowledge caused them to come back to the world to spread goodness and understanding, and to help others to find their inner Oneness.

After you have attained enlightenment, you will remain fully aware that you live in this material world and are immersed in the day-to-day problems, urges, and struggles of life. You will also remember what you have learned from your inner spirit, and you will apply it so you live your life in a godlier way.

Since the daily pressures of life will try to force your connection to the Oneness into the background, you must regularly stop and reconnect with your inner soul, your inner light, your inner direction. So, as you have learned here, keep the Sabbath. It will keep you connected to your Oneness.

Our School of Life

Even after attaining enlightenment, you will still be in this worldly existence, therefore you cannot continue to live only in pure spirit. You will discover that fact as soon as you have to eat or earn a living. Even the solitary monk living and meditating in a cave high on the mountain top must deal with the elements, forage for firewood, and find food. But he can do his chores within the light of The One. He can appreciate the sacrifices made by the animals and plants which allow him to eat. He can appreciate the gift of fire as a tool.

It is meant to be that in your Earthly life you must get along with people, obtain food, seek shelter, earn a living, and protect yourself in order to survive and thrive. Those are necessary lessons which come along with your Earthly existence. You cannot avoid them, nor should you. They are there for a reason. They are some of the more fundamental and necessary lessons you have to learn in this life in order to attain enlightenment. You cannot live life successfully without learning them.

I have come to believe that we are living this life on Earth for a reason. It is meant to be a learning experience, a training ground. It is an opportunity to learn, especially from difficulties and our mistakes, and to continuously mature, develop, and grow. This life is a school through which we learn to gain greater insight into ourselves and our connection to all. Our graduation comes when we have entered full spiritual enlightenment.

Why do I think that life is a training ground? Let us examine the mandatory experiences which naturally come along with this life on Earth for almost everyone. That might give us a hint as to this life's purpose.

The vast majority of people grow up having parents and siblings. Almost all people have to learn to love and accept their siblings. That is difficult. Siblings are very different from one another. Each has different attitudes towards life and living, and different values. Sibling rivalry and conflict is the norm, not the exception. But they are family, and humans have an inborn genetic affinity for family for good reason.

We grow up with our siblings and with our sibling rivalries. One of our earliest lessons in life is to learn to constantly get along with a close person who has different urges, likes, dislikes, and temperament. It is meant to be. We learn from it. We are meant to learn from it. We must learn from it. We have no choice. It is a necessary part of our Earthly life, and that is a good thing. We are working toward Oneness. That is the first step in learning to accept and love other people. Most of us eventually learn to look beyond our differences with our siblings in order to maintain the family and because we love them. At the very least, we do it because our love for our own children creates in us a desire to not deprive them of the love of family.

As you get older, it is a requirement of life that you try to learn to get along with neighboring children. You gain best friends whom you love. Through that love you learn to accept faults in your friends. You are learning about love and about life. These are required courses in the school of life.

From our parents we learn the most fundamental things, such as love, security, and happiness. My mother loved me with a wonderfully pure love. That is the love with which I love my children and my grandchildren. I am so thankful for that. They, and their children and grandchildren, will pass on that love forever.

I am grateful for my family experience. I feel terrible for those unfortunate children who grow up in tumultuous, insecure, abusive, or unloved families. They have a far greater burden than I. They have to learn love and security without having had the benefit of receiving it from their parents. It is no wonder that they often end up repeating the mistakes of their parents and/or living a life in jail or in turmoil. They are not only hurt directly by their parents as a result of their parents acting from their own genetic and epigenetic tendencies, but since they often inherit the same genetic and epigenetic tendencies as their parents, their parents' behavior toward them triggers and reinforces their own internal sensitivities. What a shame. That is a situation where there should be intervention. There should be a way of stopping the sins of the parents from being visited upon their children into successive generations. It has not successfully happened yet. I hope it will soon. Such a solution needs empathy and judgment.

Your children have their own thoughts, desires and goals, and you as their parent cannot impose yours upon them. You can teach them patience and wisdom through your actions, and you can give them knowledge. But your greatest gift to them is your love which will live through them into life everlasting.

My attitude toward the spiritual was passed on to me by my father. My father taught me that God is wherever we are, not confined to some tabernacle somewhere. He also taught me to think for myself. He often said," Nothing is impossible." What a wonderful lesson. A lesson which I always understood as being inspirational, not literal.

Since those lessons described above seem to be a necessary part of almost everyone's life on Earth, could it be that we live on Earth in order to progressively learn greater and greater love and attain higher and higher levels of consciousness? First, we learn to love our parents, then our siblings, friends, and then life's acquaintances. Then perhaps all of humanity, including those who have harmed us. We then use what we have learned to love and accept others. All in all, love your parents, siblings, friends, strangers, and the people who have wronged you. You will then feel Universal Love.

In its progression from separateness to Oneness, your soul has had to progress through the stages of awareness, from its time as a one-celled organism to its present state as a human being. Through all those stages of consciousness, it has always identified itself as being its physical form. That progression has been good, not bad. The ego's growth, through its interaction with its surrounding physical world, has allowed it to survive and evolve until it has now reached a highly evolved human form. It is now time to graduate beyond the egoistical identification with the physical body into a higher consciousness. Your next evolutionary leap!

Your final stages of consciousness involve seeing through the veil of physicality and realizing that your spirit is in fact not its physical body. That your body is merely a vehicle through which you interact with the physical world. When you see through your veil of physicality, you can see beyond to your true being, your true spirit. Thus continues your journey along The Path.

Using your newfound spiritual understanding, you will continue to learn life's many lessons as you navigate through your Earthly existence. The unavoidable trials and tribulations from which life brings you, and the necessary lessons you will continue to learn from that will help you further along your spiritual path. Needless to say, there will be bumps in the road. But you will continue to grow and become wiser from them. Your path will contain meanderings and stagnant pools along the way as does a river, but it will travel on as do you.

You will eventually learn to refrain from succumbing to preconceived notions and knee-jerk reactions, and will grow to observe things, ideas, emotions, problems, and painful experiences with an objective, aware eye. You will observe how they are unfolding and will observe how your view of them affects how they unfold. You will become more whole by letting yourself learn from the bad as well as the good. You won't be afraid of it, or deny it.

You will accept the presence of your negative emotions and reactions and will accept both the good and the bad that is part of your ego. You will not allow them to control you. You have seen the truth. Remember: The One within you is not binary. It is not one thing or another. It is all. It incorporates all of the good and all of the bad. And you will discover that there is a purpose to it all.

Seeing the Beauty Within the Paths of Others

Hopefully, through this teaching you will find The Path which facilitates your journey toward The One. You must remember that you must not let your path be a means of separation from other paths or other people. If that happens, you should realize that you are moving away from your true path, which is away from your true self. Your true path is that which unifies with all paths.

Focusing on the differences between your path and theirs will cause you to become sidelined from your journey to The One within you. You must first recognize that you have deviated from your true path, and must veer back to the commonality, the Oneness. This requires that you do not look with disdain upon people who practice things which seem mundane. Listen to them, and seek to learn of the things of value they get from those practices. Remember that different people are at different places along their journey to awakening, and they connect with their spirit in different ways.

Even intellectually challenged people feel and love. They have life purposes. If those purposes involve loving and/or helping others, how can you denigrate them? Look at yourself in the mirror and truthfully judge how well you have done at those fundamental and important life challenges. Don't spend your time and effort denouncing other people's faults. Spend your time and effort correcting your own!

Relish in the beauty of the different paths that others have taken. Make sure to share your experiences with others, and seek to learn of the common aspects of your paths. Also recognize that the common aspect of all paths is where you will find the infinite One within yourself and others. Seek to discover the commonness of the different paths. That is The Path to God, spiritual enlightenment, and pure awareness.

Revel in the beauty within the paths of others because by appreciating their beauty you will better appreciate your own beauty. Touch the common denominator of humanity and you will feel that connection. It is the love through which you appreciate the universe, the Oneness that is God.

Identification with a separate group by race, creed, nation, or gender to the rejection or denigration of another is the cause of discord and unhappiness. The love of, and fascination with, the beautiful differences among people is what will make you individually happy and respected, and make you sow peace and happiness in general. Seeing life through the eyes of many people will make it more three-dimensional for you and thus easier for you to conceptualize.

Seeing the Essential Goodness Within All People

Unlock your heart. Allow your love to come forth. Trying to make yourself seem better at the expense of others will surely lead to your dissatisfaction and failure. You are a greater, happier person when you uplift others. Don't you really know that truth deep down within your heart?

Haven't you experienced that when you express anger or hate, anger and hate seem to come back at you. Haven't you experienced that when you give love, love is more likely to be given back to you? That's because when you give love to others, it can awaken the love within them. This is true even when they initiate hate toward you. You can stop the hateful cycle by giving love in return.

Instead of being made insecure by the past negative acts of others, you will not let those internal memories and primitive emotions control you, rule over you, or make you feel inadequate, insecure, afraid, suspicious, jealous, angry, confused, or hurt in any way. You will instead recognize that the hurtful acts of people against you so long ago were beyond the control of those people. They were victims just as you were. You and they are in the same boat.

Just as you will look objectively at your own irrational negative reactions, you will understand the reactions of others and forgive them. You will forgive them, just as you would have them forgive you. You will forgive because you have seen the futility and self-destructiveness of feeling hatred. You will know that forgiveness is not just what you give to others, it is a gift you give to yourself. It is your liberation, your redemption.

Your wisdom and judgment must come from your loving spirit. It must look at life's experiences from the standpoint of love and not just from intellect. There must be cooperation and harmony between your intellect and spirit. Your intellectual mind can work with your loving spirit in order to accomplish helpful actions on Earth and fulfill your life's purpose. Your intellectual mind must, however, follow the lead of love.

How can the suicide bombing of multitudes of adults and children in the name of God come from love? Even if the bombers feel those people have committed or condoned evil, is evil the way to end evil? Love is the way to end evil. A cycle of evil will continue to beget evil until it is ended through love.

Harmony of mind and spirit is the way to live a spiritual life. Love and reason become fused into a holy union, and create a higher form of consciousness.

Even bad acts are not totally evil. Perhaps they are subconsciously done out of perceived fear, jealousy, lust, or anger. They may be done by an otherwise good person. Put yourself in their place. You have been there. How would you want someone to think about you? In the material world of duality, nothing is purely good or purely bad. They are merely degrees upon a continuum.

Love cuts through those perceptions. Through love you can see the essential goodness within a person who has committed a bad act. Through love you see beyond good and bad to the true spirit within. You see through the veils created by your ego and those of others.

Unhappiness comes from disappointed expectation. If you expect another person to act so as to satisfy your expectations of them, you will be disappointed and thus unhappy. If you do not expect someone else to satisfy your own needs, you will not be unhappy because of them. You should be happy when they are happy. When they satisfy their own desires!

Accept the Beauty and Impermanence of All

Relying upon something staying as you know it is a losing proposition. Change is inevitable in the physical universe. The future is constantly being remade by the progression of events. Things in front of your eyes in this instant are already fading out of existence and being replaced by something else.

You must realize that the present is only a split second in eternity. Rely upon your inner spirit, which is the only true reality. It should be your reference point from which decisions are made.

So, do not make decisions based upon jealousy, pride, anger, things you wish you had, or what you wish you were. These are the transitory, shallow things that will bring you no satisfaction or happiness. They involve self-deceit. Instead, be modest. Be kind, gentle, and truthful. Be patient and tolerant.

Becoming rich should not be your goal. It can, however, be a result from a drive to help others or society, or to do or make something better. Not for unlimited money. If you do it solely for the money, you will make self-destructive mistakes. You will cut corners, or hurt others. You will not be admired even by those enveloped in the same self-deception. Look how many rich people have lost their marriages. They gave up love for money. The false god. The golden calf.

Be careful that the thing that makes you comfortable does not become your chain. It may be limiting your life. Allow yourself to open to a freer, less judgmental place.

Look beyond your initial impression of an act, or a thing. See its true components and its real origins. Then, you will be able to make wise decisions about it.

Don't worry about the future. Do good now and the future will be the natural result that follows sooner or later.

Meditation will make you open to and aware of the moment. Everything is allowed to be in the moment. Every moment. If you take care of the moment, the years will take care of themselves.

Be fully aware of each present moment just as it is, and accept that it is always evolving. That will allow you to live your life more fully.

The harm that comes from other people can only harm you if you let it. If you see that it comes from pain within them, then you can only pity them and not be hurt. If you let your kindness–your empathy–come forth, you will try to help them in a kind and loving manner. If they are so steeped in their misery that they still refuse your help, what can you do? Just go on with your life uninjured.

What if they harm your reputation with others? You will find that if you maintain and exhibit your loving kindness attitude toward your aggressor, other people will respect you and give you the benefit of the doubt. If you react from anger or desperation, they will not really know who to believe. Will they see a manifestly negative person versus a holy person, or two people who are wrapped up in revenge and anger?

Always speak with truth, appropriateness, and kindness, and remember that silence is sometimes the most appropriate form of speech. Harsh speech sends a ripple of hurt through the universe, whereas kind speech can change hurt into healing.

Do not feel that it is somehow unholy or hypocritical to receive. You should become aware that by receiving you bless the giver. Do not be so proud or selfish as to deprive the giver of your blessing. Life is a flow, and if you perpetually give without receiving, you dam the flow. As you receive, give; and as you give, receive. There cannot be charity without need, nor can there be success without trial.

Be happy for what you have. Consider the history of people who have lost their limbs, sight, or movement. See how they have modified their life to become just as happy and fulfilled as before their misfortune. As a matter of fact, see how so many of them have actually had their lives improved as a result of the misfortune.

Make the most of your life no matter its condition. What else do you have? Make the most of what you have. You need look no further than the life of Stephen Hawking, the astrophysicist who wrote *A Brief History of Time*. Who could live a fuller and more meaningful life than that man who was in a wheelchair and who could not speak, or even gesture?

Don't be a victim of events. Be above all that. You are in control of your own life, your own destiny. Live your life's purpose. What-ever is thrown at you in life, make the most of your life. What else can you do?

Think of it this way. Whatever happens is meant to happen. This life on Earth is a school through which we human souls learn gradu-ally to become transcendent, holy, blissful, immortal, and eternal. To become unified with all that there is, is NOT NOTHING. It is EVERYTHING! That is your destiny. Do not inhibit it. Let it happen.

Remember that all you leave behind is your impact on the world, especially upon your fellow human souls. Cast your goodness upon the waters. Teach your children and grandchildren with your actions and disposition; not just your words. They watch you as you deal with your misfortunes, and what they see will affect their lives. And then their lives will affect the lives of those who follow them. How you live your life will be a legacy that follows you. That will be your immortality. Do not fail it.

Do not succumb to the inevitable misfortunes of life. Overcome them. Rise above them. That actually happens naturally and easily when you have come to understand the nature of life.

You are One with all there is. You are not a leaf to be battered about by the wind. The wind and the leaf are a part of you. You are beyond all of those miniscule, unstoppable events of life on Earth. You can look down upon them with interest and empathy, just as you would look upon the interactions of toddlers at play. You have risen above being controlled by the innumerable events of the world. You have gained the wisdom to see the inner nature of all through under-standing it all.

And now you automatically love it all. You love the world, and all that is in it, as you love yourself. You forgive your child's foolish actions because you know the goodness which lies behind those immature actions.

Merging the Spiritual and the Material

You are in a material body for a good purpose. Use your material body to manifest your higher spiritual understanding. Once you become enlightened, you will not reject your material life. You will use material things in furtherance of spiritual ideals. Live your life's purpose.

You will bring an enlightened attitude to all of life. You will become immersed in activities of the world in order to further your enlightened goals. You will fuse your infinite spirit with the material world in order to relieve suffering, protect the weak and downtrodden, further brotherhood among all, and bring love, happiness, and spiritual advancement to humanity.

While doing so, you must be wary of becoming again susceptible to illusory desires and primal emotions. That is why you must regularly and frequently become still and connect purely with the spiritual love within yourself.

Retreating temporarily to a life of solitude apart from the world, such as meditating, or retreating to a desert or mountain for the purpose of contemplating what you have learned, is a good thing. But permanently separating yourself can be out of fear or denial of aspects of your material life, and may not be the path to illumination.

When you commence your life and live your daily existence within your spiritual path, you will hopefully remember all of the spiritual lessons you have learned. You will discover that you can live in your true spirit while traveling the world. You will keep the light of your true spirit burning as you travel through life. It will keep you pointed in your true direction and be a guiding light to help you light up the world with your continence. You will optimize your presence on Earth and live your life's true purpose.

You will welcome your new insight, but you also have to walk The Path. You will not really make progress until you traverse life with both your revelations and your heart. Let your new insights guide you, and let your heart give you the drive to walk that walk.

Applying your revelations through your worldly actions makes them your own, makes them more real, and implants them more securely within your heart. Kahlin Gibran said in *The Prophet*: "... your body is the harp of your soul." What this means is let your hands act from The One and let your mouth speak from The One. Make your words become the voice of eternity passing through your mouth. Let your countenance become a light shining upon all. Leave love and truth along your trail so that all benefit from it.

HOPE IN THE TIME OF COVID

As I finish this book, I find my attention drawn to this momentous time in which we have lived. It could truly be called an event of biblical proportions. I am finishing this book just as we seem to be emerging from the COVID pandemic..

Little did I know over the years as I was writing this book, that my description of life as a training ground for the learning of the unity of all humanity would become so obviously true during this time. This has been a time of testing humanity.

In the early days of the pandemic, as I saw what was going on in the world, I had hoped that it would force people to stop and reflect upon what was truly important. I had hoped the pandemic would bring all of us together, because truly we are all in this together. Some did, but our divisions won out in the hearts of many. Mask versus no mask. Restrictions to prevent the virus from spreading versus the freedom to act carelessly and infect ourselves or others. In the United States, the president could have brought us together but he chose to pit us against one another.

A number of events also collided during this time. Police shootings of Black people not guilty of capital crimes caused people of all ethnicities to rise up by the hundreds of thousands. There were great marches in the streets, and also some rioting by comparatively fewer people whose anger and frustration conquered their wisdom. It reminded me of the 1960s, when the young people of the United States arose in the streets and campuses because they were being forced to give up their lives for a war which they knew was wrong.

But as said earlier in this book: the world is no doubt unfolding as it should. There is a reason why the day is darkest before the dawn.

The human soul, when finally recognizing itself as being on the brink of utter disaster, can finally become disillusioned with its prior assumed path. It can correct itself before it is too late.

Hopefully the marches in the streets, and even the rioting, will bring about a realization that Black lives really do matter as much as White lives. Hopefully the violent insurrection at the nation's Capitol on January 6, 2021, which included the attempted overthrow of democracy has shown the extremists and the intentionally gullible that hate and division is a life badly lived, and that it can end in devastation. Hopefully the United States, having come so close to losing its democracy, will now cherish it more than it has for decades, and no longer take it for granted.

In the midst of all of this pain, something big did happen within the United States of America. After years of ever-increasing division and hate, America was forced to look itself in the mirror. It had stepped from years of hate and dissidence onto the edge of a precipice it now recognized as the coming catastrophic end of the democracy it cherished. As a result, the majority of the population chose to elect a president who was a man exhibiting faith, empathy, and goodness, a man who espoused unity among all people. Let us hope that he successfully continues to travel that path, and that the people still immersed in fear, hatred, and division do not sabotage his efforts to bring us all together as one. Hopefully they too at some point will recognize that they stood at the precipice of disaster.

The year 2020 was a blessing in other ways as well. It forced us to leave our busy day-to-day life and to exist only in the moment. We could make no plans for the future, and for the first time in our lives, we actually found ourselves contemplating that our future could end with only two weeks' notice. So, making the most of every moment became necessary, perhaps for the first time in our lives.

We were forced to have limitless patience. Food ordered from the market would not arrive for days or weeks, and much of it would be unavailable or substituted for something less desirable. We could not find toilet paper. We were forced into isolation in order to save our lives. We could have no in-person social interaction, even with our closest friends or family members outside of our physical households. And there was little or nothing we could do about it. Impatient people had to learn patience. We were forced to be only in the present moment all day every day. All plans had stopped. There were no expectations of us. No appointments. No certainty.

We could have found it pleasant and calming. We could have taken a deep breath and settled into the calmness, instead of being antsy about doing things we could not do anyway.

The state into which the year 2020 put all of us dominated our existence. Our life was forced to revolve around the effects of the pandemic. Consider that it affected everyone in the world more or less equally. Everyone on Earth was now in the same place, worrying about the same things, focused on the same things. All of humanity was all together in the same boat for the first time in generations, maybe for the first time in its entire history.

We were forced to self-isolate so that we wouldn't get infected, or infect others. If others became infected, our chances of becoming infected were higher. This is a practical example of all humanity being together, and every life being dependent on all other lives. If ever there was a time when all humanity could come together, that was it. Politics and other Earthly issues could be pushed far into the background. It could have put all of humanity dramatically further along the path to enlightenment.

Living through the time of COVID transformed our lives into lives different than they had ever been. Our Earthly lives were now fundamentally changed. What a perfect opportunity to reflect upon our lives which could end in days with little warning. We could have reflected upon what is most important in our lives. We could have decided to not put off those most important things.

It was a good opportunity to consider the here and now, the only place where we then found ourselves. Being in the present; only in the now. Recognizing all full well after this experience that the past is truly only a distant memory, and that the future is something upon which we cannot rely.

But here we are still in a transitional period. The pandemic has lessened, yet it might come back with a fury. We don't know. Our lives are no longer suspended. We can again hug our parents and grandchildren. We can travel. We can shop. We can now enter the insides of a crowded establishment. But are we truly safe?

We can plan. We no longer must seriously consider that we could die within the next week or two without warning. We have looked into the face of the possibility of imminent death and most of us have survived

How many of us have taken this opportunity to reflect and grow? To focus on those things most important to us? The pandemic gave us the precious time of which we always lamented we did not have. Well, now that you had unlimited time, what did you make of it?

This time could still be a transitional period for you. You can still make the time to pause and think about your life. If you previously had felt downtrodden or insecure, the pandemic made everyone feel downtrodden and insecure. The field has been leveled for you. The pandemic was the great equalizer. You can now take the opportunity to start a fresh new life.

You have discovered that less is more. Having had less to do left room for the often hidden peaceful and silent aspects of your life to come forth. You now can better appreciate the simplest of things and do the most important of things. You now know enough to open up to all the small miracles which you had been rushing by without noticing. Now is your time to gaze upon the burning bush and contemplate its meaning.

CONTINUING ON MY PATH

As for myself, I am on The Path and continue to advance spiritually. If there is a complete permanent escape from ego while still in this earthly life, I have not yet merged with it. Generally, while living my earthly life I do not know anywhere close to all of the answers. However, during those glorious periods when I have been within The One, I did have full awareness, universal consciousness and absolute understanding. Every time I have been within The One my life has improved. I know that I am not yet solidly one with The One, but I know it is worthwhile and wonderfully rewarding to stay on The Path. I am a work in progress.

I will continue on the Path, and be happy with every minute of it. When the misfortunes of life create reactive feelings of frustration and anger within me, I soon enough remember the lessons learned from my moments within The One. I remember that my happiness comes from responding to hate, ignorance and callousness with love and empathy.

If I do find a permanent and stable escape from the control of ego in this lifetime, I will share it with you. I am gratified each time I observe myself being urged by my ego to do something reactive and then catch myself and allow my better angels to take over.

As you read books by other people about spiritual enlightenment, you'll see them using different names for what I call The One. For example, God, Being, awareness, and others. I have thought about which helps me best understand the ultimate experience, but I have found that the more I consider the different names the further I get from that experience. I am reminded by myself to listen to my own advice to forget the names, because different names and different forms just bring us further from The One.

I have also made the mistake of trying to fully understand the relationship of The One to our own internal spirit, and why it is that way. My lesson so far from that experience is that that exercise confuses me. We should just accept this miracle of our spirit without thinking about it. Thinking is the trap set by our egoistic minds to try to block us from merging with our pure spirit.

When I become complacent and think that I know what I am talking about, reality sticks me in the eye. Such as when I rely upon my faith in a close friend or relative and then have them say or do something that undermines that faith. I am struck that I was starting again to take this path for granted.

And so, it appears again. This continuing school of life. I relearn that I should accept and even expect the unexpected, and that I must have enough faith in the humanity of others to not allow an action or statement to question my love for them. My faith in them will apparently have to continue to evolve, accepting aspects of them which I will continue to learn. Accepting them as they are, not as I hope they are or expect them to be. And each time that happens I learn more about what I think I already know. I understand more deeply what I think I already fully understand.

I find that I have to keep learning over and over again the things I teach here. It is so easy to lose it in our busy, complex lives. But every time I stop and meditate, the revelation comes back to me, and at that moment I glow with happiness. It is like falling in love over and over again.

I am patient along The Way. I know that epiphanies will come when I am ready for them. Greater and greater understanding continues to come to me while I read books written by spiritually enlightened people, or when I still my worldly mind and open myself to the calm beauty which emerges. It is when I am within that beautiful stillness that the spiritual wisdom deep within me takes me over and opens me to the awareness of the Oneness of all.

As for you, please continue your progress along The Path, because The Path does not end. As you travel, always maintain your loving heart and your openness to new ideas. Remember to accept change. Yes, you will have setbacks. But it is how you deal with setbacks that defines you.

Regretfully I must end this book. Every time I read it or think about it, more ideas come into my head. I have been incorporating these ideas into this book for many, many years, but there is a time when one thing must end so that something else can begin.

I have taken many notes of more ideas, but they will have to wait for another book, or some other form of communication. So "stay tuned," as they say. I am still a human in the physical world, so you can expect me to continue to search. My future experiences will no doubt cause my understanding of The One to evolve.

I welcome the thoughts and experiences of my readers, so that through the sharing of our revelations we can all further expand our paths. If you are interested in my new realizations, revisions of my current ideas, or just learning what I continue to learn, you should go to my website TedOrenstein.com and sign up for my newsletter, and while there visit my blog. I will let you know of my new ideas and realizations, and I will also welcome the input of other serious searchers. I look forward to working together to share our experiences and to learn from one another.

MEDITATION BASICS

(This can be copied and used as a reminder when you want to begin meditating)

- Sit in a place and in a way as to minimize the diversion caused by aches and pains. Use a cushion if doing so helps you focus or be more comfortable. Sit with good posture and an erect spine.
- Now focus upon your breath. Close your eyes and begin to breathe deeply, slowly and steadily. Breathe through your nose.
- Breathe in four to six seconds and four to six seconds out. Breathe in for a long four to six counts, then breathe out for a long four to six counts. Be conscious that you are inhaling and exhaling deep breaths. Breathe in until your abdomen expands. Then breathe out all the air from your lungs, remaining conscious that you are exhaling. When you breathe out, feel your abdomen contract. Continue to focus on each breath, in and out.
- While you are breathing, be sure to keep your back straight and your head and neck aligned with your spinal column. Relax all the muscles in your hands, arms, shoulders, back, and legs.
- Stay focused on your breath instead of your thoughts. Consider counting your breaths. Or you can substitute a spiritually enhancing phrase or chant; saying it as you breathe out.

- Be relaxed but alert. Alert to the moment, not to what has happened in the past, and not to what you want to happen in the future.
- Ignore outside stimuli. As you sit in stillness, your mind will try to interfere. Just recognize it for what it is. It is your mind trying to interfere. As Earthly distractions creep in, be aware of them, but don't let them take hold of you. Acknowledge them, but know they are not you. You might think, "Oh, a distraction just crept in." Just accept that it can be there without interfering with your focus on your breathing. Don't get involved with it. Just go back to focusing on the feel of your breath going in and out, in and out. Return to the stillness.
- Keep focusing on your deep, steady breathing, and a calm will eventually come over you.
- Just be still, and open yourself up. Keep breathing deeply, slowly, and steadily. Free your mind. Don't think.
- Concentrate on your breath. Breathe in and out, in and out. There is no set timeframe. Breathe until a calmness comes over you and you feel like you are floating.

<u>Thoughts to Keep Close as You Travel Your Life's Path</u>

(This can be copied and kept for easy reference)

Appreciate the little things in life. The crust on bread, the richness of ripe fruit, the joy of a child, the rustling of grass or leaves in the wind, and the calmness of a beautiful landscape.

Do not sacrifice the long term and deep for the short term and superficial. Keep your holy character as you deal with the world. Don't let evil suck you in.

No matter how long you have been practicing mindfulness or where you are on your path to enlightenment, you will experience happiness and sadness, gain, and loss. How it affects you will depend upon what you see in it and your perception of it.

Accept all that comes into your life, including misfortunes such as sickness and death. They, as you know, are usually unavoidable. Learn from them. That is why they are a part of life. Appreciate what you learn from them.

You must realize that the present is only a split second in eternity. Rely upon your inner spirit, which is the only true reality. It should be your reference point from which decisions are made.

Relying upon something staying as you know it is a losing proposition. Change is inevitable in the physical universe. The future is constantly being remade by the progression of events. Things in front of your eyes in this instant are already fading out of existence and being replaced by something else.

Those things that bother and worry you really have no hold upon you. They will change before your very eyes. They will soon not be the same as they are now, but will alter and eventually cease to exist. The things that trouble you about them are only a product of your perception and attitude. They are delusions you allow yourself. See beyond those delusions.

Instead, turn obstacles into fuel for improvement. An obstacle can either overwhelm you, or you can use it as a learning experience.

Learn from that experience. It all depends on how you look at it, your perception of it. Do you see it as being huge and unconquerable, or do you see it as a challenge from which you can learn?

Don't deny, avoid, or hide your grief. It is important that you go through it. After immeasurable despair, you will learn from it. Allow your painful experience to open yourself to a greater awareness.

When you are within the darkness of loss and despair, meditate so that your inner all-knowing spirit will illuminate your tormented soul. It will show you how your loss can be filled, and your despair can be cured. Not by you receiving something, but by you truly realizing that you already have what you feel is missing. It will show you how to perceive all that you already have and how to realize its full importance.

If you choose to not be hurt by insults and other slights from others, then you will not be hurt. If you do not feel hurt, you have not been hurt. It is up to you!

You can rise above the twists and turns of banal existence. It is the world as it is, but you can accept it and deal with it. You can be successful in the midst of adversity.

A positive aspect of being within the depths of despair is the knowledge that the only direction from there can be up. If your life has been in darkness, it is within your power now — at this moment — to light your candle. It is never too late to start your journey.

A person who has attained spiritual enlightenment can see both pain and gain within each other. Pain is a part of gain because the inevitable loss of gain can cause pain. So, every gain will eventually include loss if you let it, and every loss can end up with gain if you allow it. They are inseparable. Maintain a happy contentment by keeping the long-term in your thoughts. Know that gain and loss are both temporary. They both flow through you.

Just because it is fate does not mean it was decided long ago or has been set in stone. The trajectory of fate is forever bending by events and actions, man-made or not. Fate is forever changing. Your job is to be ready for it. Be ready to trim those sails to make positive use of the wind, no matter what speed or direction it takes.

The Ultimate Reality treats birth and death in the same way. They are both expressions of life. Although opposite, they evoke similarly profound extreme emotions. Accepting each as a part of the inevitable flow of life will give you a more balanced and profound understanding of them both.

Once you realize that you are universal and limitless, and that your life is not limited by the mere death of your physical body, you will be ready for death, and, ironically, you will be ready to lead a more content and full life. You will do everything as if it were the last thing you are doing in life. Once you are ready for death, you are ready for life.

Even the intellectually challenged person feels and loves. They also have life purposes. If those purposes involve loving and/or helping others, how can you denigrate them? Look at yourself in the mirror and truthfully judge how well you have done at those fundamental and important life challenges. Don't spend your time and effort denouncing other people's faults. Spend your time and effort correcting your own.

Relish in the beauty of the different paths that others have taken. Share your experiences with others, and seek to learn of the common aspects of your paths. Know that the common aspect of all paths is where you will find the infinite One within yourself and others. Seek to discover the commonness of the different paths. That is The Path to God, spiritual enlightenment, and pure awareness.

Always speak with truth, appropriateness, and kindness, and remember that silence is sometimes the most appropriate form of speech. Harsh speech sends a ripple of hurt through the universe, whereas kind speech can change hurt into healing.

You should always remember to be guided by The Golden Rule which is, "Do unto others as you would have them do unto you." The basis of that is stated clearly, simply, and profoundly in Leviticus: "Love your neighbor as yourself." But you have learned to do something even more difficult, yet more important: "Love your enemy as yourself."

Put yourself in the other person's shoes. You are not always the best person you can be, are you? But in spite of that, hopefully others still accept you and like you. So, do not be quick to judge others. Give them the benefit of the doubt.

Keep an open mind. Ask questions and listen in addition to saying things. When you say things, you are only repeating what you already know. When you ask questions and listen, you can learn new things.

Always speak with truth and kindness. When you say things which are hurtful to others, not only do you hurt them, but you also create a nasty atmosphere which comes back to hurt you as well. Be kind, even when someone has been hurtful to you. You can be the one who changes an unhappy atmosphere into a happy one. You can do that.

Always be comfortable with who you are, and secure and content within yourself. It is feelings of insecurity and lack of contentment which cause jealousy, fear, and anger to emerge.

Try not to react immediately to your first impression of something. Think about it. Sleep on it and see how you feel the next day. Consider its deeper meaning and its effects. If you do that, your response will be wiser. And remember that sometimes silence can be the wisest response.

When you consider your life's goals, think of the greater good. Doing things for selfish reasons always lessons them.

ABOUT THE AUTHOR

Ted Orenstein writes, speaks, and teaches about spiritual enlightenment. He enjoys sharing with others that there is a purpose and direction to the universe and that it is good. A former lawyer, Ted's mission is to help others find greater meaning and fulfillment, and a deeper understanding of why people are what they are.

For more information or to contact the author, go to tedorenstein.com

NOTES

2. My Journey

1. Richard Maurice Bucke, *Cosmic Consciousness: A Study in the Evolution of the Human Mind* (Philadelphia: Innes and Sons)

3. Finding Spiritual Enlightenment

1. Chaim Stern, *Gates of Repentance: The New Union Prayerbook for the Days of Awe*, New York: Central Conference of American Rabbis

4. What Is God?

1. Robert Eno, *The Analects of Confucius,* 12.2 & 15.24, https://scholarworks.iu.edu/dspace/handle/2022/23420
2. Jeffrey Moses, *Oneness, Great Principles Shared by All Religions*, by Jeffrey Moses, New York: Ballantine Books
3. Devi Bhagavatam, Canto 11, Chapter 2
4. Meriam-Webster Encyclopedia of World Religions, p. 462
5. *The Analects of Confucius: Book 1*
6. *I Ching,* appended remarks 2.5
7. Published by Warner/Chappell Music, Inc.
8. *Bhagavad Gita*, 4.11
9. Chaim Stern, *Gates of Repentance*, New York: Central Conference of American Rabbis
10. Deut. 6:4
11. *Mishnah Torah*, Chapter One, Halachah 7
12. Shinichi Hisamatsu and Hyung Woong Park, "Zen and the Various Acts," *Chicago Review* 12, no. 2 (1958), https://www.jstor.org/stable/25293451
13. Thich Nhat Hanh, *Living Buddha, Living Christ*, New York: Riverhead Books.
14. "De Officiis," Marcus Tullius Cicero

5. Where Do We Look to Find that Oneness?

1. *Gates of Repentance*, Ibid, p. 254
2. Paraphrased and summary of pp. 31-35 in *Living Buddha, Living Christ* by Thich Nhat Hanh, Riverside Books
3. Karen Armstrong, *The Spiral Staircase*, New York: Anchor Books

4. #12 from "Gitanjali" by Rabindranath Tagore, the brilliant Bengali poet and Nobel laureate.
5. Robert Alfred Vaughn, *Hours with the Mystics*, Volume 1, New York: Charles Scribner's Sons
6. Ninian Smart, *The Religious Experience of Mankind*, New York: Charles Scriber & Sons
7. Ibid p. 469
8. Ibid. p. 518
9. Ibid p. 519
10. Ibid pp. 520-21
11. "Summa Theologiae," I.13.11
12. Luke 17:21
13. Marcus Aurelius in *Meditations*, p. 38, as translated by Gregory Hays, New York: The Modern Library
14. Rachel Yehuda, PhD and Linda M. Bierer, MD, "The Relevance of Epigenetics to PTSD: Implications for the DSM-V," PMC of US National Library of Medicine, National Institutes of Health, 2009, https://www.ncbi.nlm.nih.gov/pmc/articles/PMC2891396/
15. Numbers 14:18

6. How to Find the Oneness Within Yourself?

1. Luke 17: 20-21.
2. John 1836.
3. Albert Einstein, *Living Philosophies*, New York: AMS Press.
4. Maharishi Manesh Yogi, *The Science of Being and Art of Living*, London: International SRM Publications
5. p. 101
6. Karen Armstrong, *The Spiral Staircase*, New York: Anchor Books
7. Herbert Fingarette, *Confucius:The Secular as the Sacred*, New York: Harper Torch Books
8. Ibid, p. 293.
9. Ibid, pp. 278 and 293
10. Quran Part II
11. J.D. McClatchy, *The Complete Works of Henry Wadsworth Longfellow*, Library of America
12. New York, Alfred A. Knopf 1923, p. 50

7. How Will You Know When You Have Found Spiritual Enlightenment?

1. *The Complete Works of Saint John of the Cross: Volume 1 of 2*, New York: Magisterium Press
2. Genesis 28:10-22

8. Techniques for Getting to Your Inner Spirit

1. Irene Cristofori,"Neural Correlates of Mystical Experience," *Neuropsychologia*, 2016, https://pubmed.ncbi.nlm.nih.gov/26631541/
2. Exodus 19:18
3. Tao Te Ching
4. Abraham Joshua Heschel, *Man's Quest for God: Studies in Prayer and Symbolism*, New Mexico: Aurora Press

9. The Place of the True Spirit in Your Life: Finding and Living Your Life's Purpose

1. Max Ehrmann, "Desiderata," 1927
2. *The Prophet*, p. 80
3. Rabbi Alvin Fine, *Jewish Reform high holiday prayer book, Gates of Repentance*

Made in the USA
Columbia, SC
09 December 2023

28128941R00091